Things like the Truth

Things like the Truth

Out of My Later Years

Ellen Gilchrist

UNIVERSITY PRESS OF MISSISSIPPI • JACKSON

www.upress.state.ms.us

The University Press of Mississippi is a member of the Association of
American University Presses.

"Living with Light" originally written for *Shadow Patterns: Essays on Fay Jones, Architect*,
edited by Jeff Shannon (University of Arkansas Press, 2016).

"Pollen, Part II" was originally published as "Living with Sudafed" in *House and Garden*, 2008.

"My Paris and My Rome, Part II" was originally published as "Watching the Water Run" in
Smithsonian, November 2006.

"Ode to New Orleans" was originally published in *Yoga Journal*, October 2006.

"Proving Once Again I Will Do Anything for My Granddaughters" was originally published as
"Dancing Across the Waves" in *Washington Post Magazine*, March 2003.

"Being Wooed" was originally published in *Harper's Bazaar*, October 2002.

"Summer, A Memory" was originally published as "On Her Terms" in *Washington Post
Magazine*, July 2001.

"In Praise of the Young Man" was originally published in *Vogue*, September 1997.

"Christmas Past" was originally published as "Surviving the Holiday Season" in
Harper's Bazaar, December, 1994.

"Keeping Houses" was originally published in *O at Home*, Summer 2008.

First printing 2016
∞
Library of Congress Cataloging-in-Publication Data

Names: Gilchrist, Ellen, 1935– author.
Title: Things like the truth : out of my later years / Ellen Gilchrist.
Description: Jackson, Mississippi : University Press of Mississippi, [2016]
Identifiers: LCCN 2015039893 (print) | LCCN 2015051464 (ebook) | ISBN
9781496805751 (hardcover : acid-free paper) | ISBN 9781496805768 (ebook)
Subjects: LCSH: Gilchrist, Ellen, 1935—Anecdotes.
Classification: LCC PS3557.I34258 A6 2016 (print) | LCC PS3557.I34258 (ebook)
| DDC 814/.54—dc23
LC record available at http://lccn.loc.gov/2015039893

British Library Cataloging-in-Publication Data available

FOR MY CHILDREN AND THEIR CHILDREN AND THEIR CHILDREN and for all my wonderful friends and helpers. For my typist, Stephanie Meehan, and my editor, Craig Gill, and everyone who helps them be their extraordinary selves.

FOR THE HEART CANNOT LIVE WITHOUT SOMETHING TO
SORROW AND BE CURIOUS OVER.
—Eudora Welty

WHAT FAMILY HAS NO MARINER IN ITS TREE?
NO FOOL, NO FELON. NO FISHERMAN.
—Cormac McCarthy, *Suttree*

MY CREDO IS TO WRITE AS WELL AS I CAN ABOUT THINGS
THAT I KNOW AND FEEL DEEPLY ABOUT.
—Ernest Hemingway

Contents

Section Three—A Home in the Highland

Section Four—The Courts of Love

Section Five—Blessings

Mississippi, Alabama, Louisiana, Arkansas: My Southern Home

Things like the Truth

A BOOK OF ESSAYS ABOUT MY LIFE AND FAMILY AND WORK, about the aging process and the fun of fighting to stay healthy in an increasingly undisciplined culture.

This book includes a diary I wrote during my winter vacation near my family on the Mississippi coast. I am trying to learn to love the undisciplined members of my family even though they scare me because they remind me of my own undisciplined youth. I learned. I got smarter and more disciplined. So will they. I hope.

The family members I was worrying about are a man and woman, both related to me. The rest of my progeny are healthy and well and productive. But the squeaky wheel still gets the grease, as my daughter-in-law reminds me.

Since the time when I was spending sleepless nights worrying about these two, here is what has happened. The woman has gone to a new doctor and had her blood pressure medicine lowered and changed. Now she is back to her usual, wonderful, brilliant, productive self. She is well. Did it do any good for me to have worried about her? You bet it did. We send strange vibrations to people we love when we worry about them. My messages always say, I'm mad at you for harming yourself. I'm worried and can't sleep. Stop hurting yourself because it is hurting me.

The man I was worrying about was grieving for his dead father and two close friends who died in accidents they did not cause, one in an automobile, the other on an oil rig.

He went to AA meetings for two hundred days in a row, went back to church in a meaningful way and has completely recovered from the depression that caused his drinking. I know it helped him for me to worry about him. I am a logical positivist, but there are things we know that we cannot prove.

"For the heart cannot live without something to sorrow and be curious over," Eudora Welty wrote. I try to let that lead me when I am worrying about my progeny. Waking up all night worrying about your children is a losing battle but we do it whether it is wise or not. The brighter and more creative you are the harder you worry.

The thing that infuriates me is that I can't concentrate on the two dozen young men and women in my family who are beautiful and intelligent and hard working and ambitious. I love to look at them or be in their presence. I look forward to seeing them or writing to them on Facebook or just knowing they are alive.

If one of them calls and tells me her landlord forgot to pay her water bill and she woke that morning to no water, I get very wise and tell her that most of the people in the world have always and still have to walk to the river or the well and carry water home in heavy buckets. She liked that answer and told me later she thought about it and told it to people all day.

What treasures children are. How divine when you can be useful to them.

The Family

———❧———

I WOKE THIS MORNING TO THE SOUND OF SMALL VOICES MOVING toward the Christmas tree. "He ate the cookies," the four-year-old boy said. His name is Garrett.

"He was here," his seven-year-old brother, Marshall, answered. "Look at this." He squatted by a package with a large card that read, To Garrett from Santa Claus. "I knew he'd come. Grandmother Ellen talked to him last night when he was over New York City."

I got out of bed and went into the living room and sat on the sofa and watched. "Go get Momma and Daddy," Marshall said. "I want to open things."

They both left the room and returned with permission to open the overflowing stockings on the table. "We can't open presents until they get up," Garrett told me.

It was six-thirty in the morning in New Orleans, Louisiana on the twenty-fifth day of December, two thousand and nine. I put coffee on to brew, ran a comb through my tangled, blond gray hair and sat back on the sofa to watch the children tear through the things in their stockings. Then I called my brothers in Jackson, Mississippi. My brothers wake at dawn as I do, as my father did, as all the high-strung Scots with Daddy's genes always do no matter what time they go to bed. We get up with the sun. It is always safe to call my brothers on the telephone.

"I'm in a room with little people who still believe in Santa Claus," I told my older brother. "Although they noted he left half his milk."

"I've got Little Dooley's two-year-old and Aurora's girls," my brother answered. "But they're still asleep. Merry Christmas, Sister. How's your back?"

"My back's great, and so far no one has done anything to drive me crazy. Call me back when the children get up."

In our family we keep on being rich in children whether we plan for them or not. We lost a baby in the womb last year, a planned pregnancy. The identical twin baby girls my middle son lost in nineteen eighty-four were also planned. Maybe it's better to be overcome by passion or whatever you call the fact that nature wants babies and makes us have them and makes us love them. "God makes them cute so you won't kill them," a black woman told me once in a Walmart checkout line. I had commented on how beautiful her bad little boy was. He was having mall fever and was screaming his head off, something I can't help admiring in a two-year-old.

Between my brothers and myself we have fifteen children. Sometimes I wish I'd had more. When I was being cut open and sewed back up three times in five years all I wanted was a tubal ligation or some reliable means of birth control. We have all that now, but our family still keeps on delivering the babies and we keep on protecting and loving and trying not to spoil them.

What is Christmas for if you don't have small children around to wish on stars and watch you talk to Mrs. Santa Claus on the telephone to get an update on the trajectory of the sled?

If you don't have children of your own you should borrow some or visit an orphanage or at least go up to the local hospital and look at the newborns on Christmas morning. This is one of the great mysteries of life, a newborn child.

I had a wonderful time a few days before Christmas. I went to Jackson, Mississippi and sat around all evening with my brothers looking at old photograph albums of our exciting childhoods. When we were young my father was an engineer working for the Louisville Corps of Engineers. He was building levees on the Mississippi River. We didn't have much money but we had an elegant mother who had gone to an Episcopal boarding school and then studied French and home economics at the University of Mississippi. No matter how small our home it was always beautiful and tastefully decorated. My father had large, state-of-the-art cameras he used on the levees and there are hundreds of photographs of my brothers and me. We were always dressed in beautiful clothes, some of which my mother made and some that were hand-me-downs from our wealthy cousins in the delta. Looking at the old photographs my brothers and I marveled at the gorgeous ways we were dressed and at the wealth of games and sports our father was always teaching us to play. Poker, bridge, Monopoly, Chinese checkers, football, baseball, ice skating, roller skating, bicycles, horseback riding, swimming, diving, stilt walking, jack-o'-lantern making, the list could go on and on. I especially loved the huge, high swings my father would have constructed in the backyard anywhere we lived. There are dozens of photographs of me swinging so high it was like flying. I am holding dolls in my arm while swinging in many of the shots, my lace-trimmed underpants and petticoats, or in the winter, long underwear showing, and my little leather shoes which my mother and father polished every night.

I made up with my older brother for this Christmas. He's never been mad at me but I've been mad at him all our lives because he is smarter than I am. (He can do math.) And because he was my father's favorite and my paternal grandmother's favorite and because he never got mad at me and always protected me. Once, in nineteen fifty-three at Vanderbilt University, one of his fraternity brothers tried to rape me. I fought as hard as I could, kicking and biting, but I was losing the game. "Dooley Gilchrist will kill you," I finally yelled. I knew it was true and he knew it was true and he let me go and began to apologize. I didn't tell Dooley about it but I am telling him now. "It's not too late to go find 'Tony' and beat him up, Dooley, but wait until your recent eye surgery has healed."

Dooley and I had a really nice, long night talking and looking at the photographs and somehow got to talking about how much we both loved *Duane's Depressed* by Larry McMurtry. We started talking about the book and began to laugh. We laughed until tears rolled down our cheeks. My daddy used to laugh that way. I think it's a Scots thing. Scots are so serious most of the time that when they think something is funny they laugh until they cry.

We were laughing that hard without having had a single drink. Me, because I quit forty years ago and won't talk to people when they are drinking, and Dooley because he just had eye surgery and his childhood polio has returned and taken out one of his lungs and he is very interested in staying alive to see how his numberless progeny turn out. There are still grandsons and great-grandsons coming along that need to learn how to hunt pheasant and quail and deer and lions and water buffalo and other animals Dooley has been hunting all his life. He is seventy-seven years old and still manages to go on safari at least once a year.

Another good thing that happened was my middle son, who is a ship's captain who has been all over the world sailing huge vessels and catching malaria while coming around the Cape of Good Hope without enough quinine for the crew, and sailing in the China seas, and finally marrying a third-generation mariner from the Chesapeake Bay and having a beautiful little boy who looks exactly like him and is fearless and wild with wide hands and high insteps and an unstoppable life-affirming attitude. Some wives in our family say he is bad, but they are just jealous because they don't have a three-year-old boy who is a head taller than everyone in his class and laughs all the time and makes ALL THE GOALS on his soccer team and can run as fast as the wind. This middle son came home to Ocean Springs, Mississippi, last month and spent five days trying to find property to buy so he can stop being on a boat and away from his family half the year.

He has two other children who live with his Bavarian ex-wife in Munich, Germany, and come to visit twice a year. His sons are so much like him it must drive his wives crazy. He doesn't care how hard he has to work or what he has to do to support these children and I am fiercely proud of him for that. Anyway, there is a chance he is going to live near to me. He is the one who will drive me to the hospital if I get sick and he's the one who won't ever let anyone put me in a nursing home or be an invalid. Also, although he doesn't like to do it anymore, he can fix anything that is broken. He sailed a thirty-foot-long boat from Florida to Saint Croix once and when the rudder broke in a storm he made one from the seat of a dinghy and sailed the boat the rest of the way to the islands with that. Also he repaired the sail with old clothes but that's another story.

Here is a story about his three-year-old son, Sean. I came home in the middle of the afternoon on the winter equinox which is my favorite day of the year since that is when we start traveling back toward the sun and the days start getting longer. I was in a really good mood knowing the earth was traveling in the right direction and I volunteered to take the three-year-old to the park. "Get your bike," I told him. "Let's get out of here." The park was full of children but they were mostly small boys Sean's age and younger. He likes to play with older children since he is an only child and accustomed to older people. Finally a brother and sister showed up that were worth his interest. The girl was about eleven, overweight and unkempt looking, but she had a nice smile. The boy was about nine and was thin and haunted looking. Sean began to bug them, pulling their shirts on the pirate fort and taunting them. They tried to run away from him, but he kept following. Finally they left the fort and began to run all over the playground trying to elude him, but he followed them relentlessly. They decided it was funny and the race was on. For thirty minutes they ran and hid and he followed. They began to play together around a beautiful new bronze water fountain. I watched them for awhile, then went nearer to see what they were doing. Sean was sitting on top of the fountain taking drinks of water and spitting it on them. They were in hysterics they thought it was so funny. Even after I made him climb down from the fountain, he kept chasing them and trying to spit on them. I was a good grandmother and scolded him and frowned, but I don't think my heart was in it. I had just seen a three-and-a-half-year-old discover spitting. Far out.

These funny, generous, poorly dressed children played with Sean for more than an hour. As the play was winding down I walked nearer to them and thanked them for their kindness. "We have a little cousin like him," the girl said. "We're used to them."

"He comes over and undresses her Barbie dolls," the boy added. "He does it every time he comes."

"I have twelve Barbies," the girl added. "I might get another one for Christmas."

The boy laughed and climbed up on a precarious stair landing, balancing there. He was wearing a too-big tee-shirt that said BAGRAM AIR FORCE BASE, AFGHANISTAN.

"Where did you get the tee-shirt?" I asked him. "Do you know someone in the army or air force or marines?"

"Our daddy," he said. "He was there." He hung his head. "He went out on the porch and had a heart attack. He's dead."

"When he came home?" I asked. "He had a heart attack here, at home, or when he was there?"

"We don't know," they both said.

"I'll go ask my grandmother," the boy said. "She's right over there." He pointed to a large, disheveled woman my age who was standing on the steps to the pavilion leaning on a cane.

The boy and girl started running in her direction. "Oh, no," I yelled. "Please don't ask her. It's three days until Christmas. Don't remind her of that."

But it was too late. They were already beside her. I followed them as fast as I could. "Your grandchildren are wonderful," I told her. "They have been so nice to my little grandson. What kind, good children they are. I'm so glad they were here today."

She smiled the same wonderful smile the chubby girl had been smiling and I wanted to run out to a store and buy five or six collector item Barbie dolls and lay them at the girl's feet.

Sean Daniel and I walked the family down to the grandmother's old Cadillac Coup de Ville. "This is funny," I said. "Your automobile is named the same thing as this park. De Ville is the name of the Frenchman in the new statue."

"The one with the cane and the sword?" the boy asked. But the light had gone out of his face. He helped his grandmother into the driver's seat. She painfully pulled her game leg into the car and settled herself on a large chiropractor's pillow.

The girl got in the seat beside her grandmother and Sean Daniel and I stood waving until they had driven away.

"Let's go get your bicycle," I said. "Your mom and dad are coming to get you to go get some shrimp for supper. Come on. Let's see if any other children have shown up to play."

We held hands and walked back across the street and up the stairs and across the flags of six nations laid out in ceramic tiles along the sidewalk leading to the playground equipment. We walked past the beautiful new bronze water fountain made possible by a grant from the Post-Katrina Committee for Reconstruction. We walked across the handsome building which replaced the wooden reconstruction of the first French settlement in the Louisiana Territories. A moment ago Sean Daniel had been wildly chasing and spitting water on the tall handsome children of a fallen hero. Now he was alone with me, not even wondering how fun goes away so fast, comes so unexpectedly and bravely and runs so fast and hilariously to some ordained conclusion and people don't stay. Come back to the park, you yell at them and sometimes they do come back and sometimes they don't.

"Look, Sean," I said as we approached the playground. "Look at the twin girls in the pink sweaters. I bet they're your age. Let's go see if they want to play with you."

A shy girl in a pink playsuit had gingerly climbed up on the pirate ship and was standing by the dinosaur blocks.

"The other girl's up there too," Sean said, getting excited, moving faster, leaving the tragedy behind and heading toward the huge plastic pirate ship full of little girls wearing pink.

Five minutes later he was their slave. The twin girls had put him in the hold and told him to stay there. Ten minutes after that they had made the bottom of the ship into a house and he had been told to take off his jacket and use it for a blanket. They were putting him to bed. His wildness had disappeared and he was happily following any orders they gave him.

Too much metaphor, I decided. He's three-and-a-half years old, for God's sake. They can't be more than five. They have domesticated him as I watched.

The twins had come equipped with Cheetos crackers and were feeding him in his bed. I went over and sat by their mother and we talked about local politics and how horrible the property taxes had become and how beautiful little girls look in pink and how much little boys liked them and sometimes even agreed to be their slaves.

They were feeding him in the bed they had made underneath the pirate ship. He was lying flat on his back with his jacket over his arms for a blanket and they were feeding him. The oldest game in the world, being played, as we speak, all over the world, on sandy beaches and in jungles and in cardboard boxes in backyards and in garages and bedrooms and dorm rooms and closets. I was an ace at playing house. Ask any of my cousins. I was a switch hitter when it came to playing house but preferred boys. If I had to play with a girl cousin I made her be the man unless it was doctor. I was always the doctor and she was the nurse.

The sobering moment with the faded grey Bagram Air Force Base tee-shirt haunted me all day. I kept counting up my progeny and naming them and forgiving their trespasses against my conservative, proto-Victorian standards. They weren't taught those standards by the culture in which they are living or by their teachers or some of them by the women my sons marry so how can I expect anything else? I can't. I shouldn't. But, of course, I do.

Why should I care so much what they do? They are breathing. Oh, God, let them keep breathing.

We lost a five-month-old fetus a few days before Christmas. My third great-grandchild. I had a premonition about the pregnancy. Very strong, very scary. So did my granddaughter-in-law, the mother. She knew something was wrong. When they took the fetus they found it was very undeveloped. The doctor wasn't even able to tell the sex. I had thought it was a girl. The mother had an IUD for three years and had just removed it. Was that a cause? She wonders and so do I. Everything about birth and birth control and pregnancy is still so much more complicated and dangerous than we admit in the twenty-first century. My oldest son was coming a month early and was a footling, coming one foot first. Only modern medicine saved the two of us, and the nine children who were born to his wives. How wonderful that we manage to think we are in charge. At least we know there are things we know that we cannot articulate or prove.

We went to hear the children's choir at Holy Name Cathedral in New Orleans at four in the afternoon on Christmas Eve. Garrett Gilchrist Walker fell asleep in my lap and I covered him with my running vest and Jean Tyson's beautiful hand-me-down Burberry raincoat. I was charmed by the service and the hymns. Marshall Kingman Walker II, age six, also fell asleep, so for most of the service Marshall Kingman Walker I and I sat with children sleeping in our laps. Very lovely. It was cold and raining outside the cathedral. A cold front from Canada was pushing down on New Orleans but the southern winds from the Gulf of Mexico turned it into rain and pushed the cold back to the north and east. It is warm here now, and pleasant and sunny. I don't want to leave and spend the winter in Fayetteville but I will, because my Scots work ethic is as strong as southern winds or northern cold fronts and I need the money.

Hurricane, 2005, August 26:
Testimony of Grandmother Ellen

THE HURRICANE HIT NEW ORLEANS IN THE MIDDLE OF THE
night. The next day the levees broke and the Gulf of Mexico began
to pour into the town. By then my children and grandchildren from
New Orleans and the Mississippi coast were all safe in Jackson, Mississippi, and I was on my way there, driving as fast as I dared and
stopping every fifty miles to fill up with gasoline as I had heard there
was no gasoline in Jackson.

The electric lines were down and the gasoline pumps wouldn't
work and the roads were clogged with trees and debris so the refilling
trucks couldn't get to the cities.

My children's cellular phones didn't work. The cell towers had
been knocked down by the storm as it made its way up the state of
Mississippi. It also knocked down fences and hedge rows and tore
up roads and uprooted pine forests and generally turned the state
into an emergency zone. Still I kept on driving. I wanted to count
heads and fingers and toes. I wanted to give away the hundred-dollar
bills I had taken out of the bank in Fayetteville as I had also heard
the banks weren't working. No electricity, no computers, no drive-in
cash machines.

I wanted to wade in and see if I could help. I was a seventy-year-
old woman on a mission.

I was not, however, willing to stay in my brother's house with ten
other people and three Labrador retrievers, one of which was fourteen years old and belonged to my cousin Bunky. I was going to stay
in town with some friends who still had air conditioning.

At least the rains had stopped. The air was crystal clear, the skies cerulean blue, gentle cirrus clouds like sleeping angels. The town of Jackson was very quiet. The only cars that seemed to be moving were emergency vehicles, repair trucks, and an occasional police car. There were long lines at the few filling stations that still had gasoline. I was down to half a tank as the last town that had gas was near the Arkansas line east of the Greenville, Mississippi, bridge.

Jackson, Mississippi, is two hundred miles north of where the hurricane hit but it was almost closed down from tornado damage in the area.

It was late in the afternoon when I got to Jackson. I went to my friends' house and managed to get a call in to my daughter-in-law and my two oldest granddaughters. They had lost their home and all their stuff and most of their cars. They came over to my friends' house and we hugged and talked and then I took all three of them out to the mall to get clean underwear and new makeup. I know that sounds stupid but I was trying to keep them busy while we waited to hear about the fate of the small town on the Mississippi coast where they live and I have a summer house. My son was in St. Croix pulling up satellite images and calling to tell us what he could see. It was my son who told his children and ex-wife that their home was gone.

"We'll fix it," I said. "We'll get you an apartment here while we figure out what to do next. We'll get an apartment and fill it with inexpensive furniture and go from there."

My oldest grandson, their son and brother, was in Jackson with his wife and child, working at a hospital, waiting to go to medical school. At least they would all be together.

The next problem was to find my youngest son and his two daughters, who had refugeed from New Orleans to my niece's farm in Madison County, outside of Jackson.

They had spent a night with the crowd at my brother's house, then gone out to the farm where there were horses and other children.

As soon as I was dressed the next morning I picked up my daughter-in-law and granddaughters at my grandson's house and we went out to the farm to see the little girls, Abigail and Juliet, ages ten and eight.

Their mother and grandmother had ridden out the storm in a huge old stucco house in New Orleans. My son had the children for the weekend so he brought them to Jackson. His British ex-mother-in-law had refused to leave, so her daughter, the girls' mother, had stayed with her.

They ended up in a crowded hotel in the French Quarter when the police made them leave the house. From there they went to Baton Rouge for four weeks. We were glad. We didn't care what a lot of crazy British women did to prove they were British, we had the girls with us.

"No school for a week or two," I told them. "Can you stand that?"

"No kidding," the oldest one said. "I guess I'll just ride horses and play with my cousins."

They seemed to be in a good mood. My son had no idea what had happened to his small house in New Orleans. He had boarded it up and left with his children. It would be days before anyone was allowed to drive the highways to New Orleans and the coast so we were living on hearsay and television reports. Except for the satellite photos being relayed from my son in St. Croix.

The big stucco house where the little girls lived with their British mother was on high ground and had survived with little damage. A tree had fallen into the swimming pool. We heard that report from somewhere.

On the afternoon of that second day we went out and rented an apartment for my daughter-in-law and the older girls. Both of their colleges were going to be closed indefinitely. The oldest one had been at the University of New Orleans, which she disliked, and the younger one had been in a small college on the coast for two days when the storm came and blew it away.

After we rented the apartment we all, including my son and the younger girls, went out to a huge discount furniture store and bought furniture and arranged to have it delivered. Then we went to Walmart and bought pots and pans and coffee makers and sheets and towels and pillows and everything we could think of to make a home. I was not going to have my oldest granddaughters be homeless.

In the end no one ever lived in the apartment. My son with the two small daughters found a house that was being restored and offered to do some of the work if the contractor would rent it to him quickly. We moved the furniture and stuff from Walmart to that house.

The days were going by quickly from the time I arrived. So many people were having so many ideas and acting on them so quickly, I can't remember what happened when. Pierre and Abigail and Juliet moved into the house he had rented.

My daughter-in-law, Rita, took her three children and drove to Ocean Springs to inspect the ruins. She found a few pieces of Spode china and the cars upside down in a small lake formed by the tidal wave.

They were driving a Chevrolet my oldest granddaughter had rented while her car was being repaired. They ended up keeping the car for two months and the insurance company kept on paying for it. The car being repaired was a Mitsubishi Gallant I had given Ellen six months before. They had driven the rented Chevrolet to Jackson because it had the largest trunk. I had bought the Mitsubishi with money I made holding a chair in the humanities at Tulane University. I used the money to buy cars for Ellen, Aurora, Marshall, and Pierre, a humane use for money if I ever heard of one.

Since then I have been using my money to pay tuition to various colleges and medical schools and universities. I get money from a university and I give it to other universities. I am an extremely inventive economist and sometimes think I should offer my service to the United States government.

Here is the cast of characters for this Hurricane report.

Grandmother Ellen, me

Ellen Walker, my oldest granddaughter

Aurora Walker, numero dos granddaughter

Rita Walker, my brilliant daughter-in-law

Pierre Walker, my youngest son

Abigail Walker, his oldest daughter, my fourth granddaughter

Juliet Walker, numero dos daughter, my fifth granddaughter

Robert Alford Gilchrist, my younger brother, "Uncle Bob"

Robert Alford Gilchrist, "Little Bob," age eleven

Whitney Marion Gilchrist, my niece, age fifteen

Julie Brasfield Gilchrist, my wonderful, long-suffering sister-in-law

Treena Gilchrist Klaus, my niece, who lives on a horse farm with her generous and kind husband, Jimmy, and her children

Amy Klaus, twelve at time of the hurricane

Tyler Klaus, thirteen at time of the hurricane

Aunt Roberta Alford Kleinschmidt, my mother's youngest sister, who shares my sons' rare blood type and is the most outspoken of all my aunts. I loved her very much. Her home in New Orleans was destroyed so she moved, at age eighty-three, to her house on the beach in Gulf Shores, Alabama, and invited members of her Episcopal Church in Metairie to come and live with her if they had lost their homes. Many of them did. I sent her newspaper reports and got many very funny letters from her in return. If I can find any of them I will add them to this essay as an addendum. One she especially liked was a long, unnecessarily nasty article in the *New York Times* Sunday Living section about people from New Orleans moving to their second homes on the coast. I sent it to Roberta by Federal Express since mail and newspapers were not being delivered for several months after the storm.

George W. Healy, Junior, my beloved oldest first cousin, called by everyone he knows, "Bunky." He was the president of the United States Maritime Lawyers Association. I met him once in New York City where they were having a meeting and was delighted to find that everyone there called him "Bunky."

Sharon Healy, Bunky's wife, who allows him to be exactly who he is without ever trying to change him. She is from Oklahoma and my mother and Bunky's mother adored her and were so happy when Bunky settled down and made her his wife. Sharon and Bunky are the about-to-be-married couple in my short story "The Famous Poll at Jody's Bar."

Assorted Labrador retrievers, Prestidigitation, Dooley, and Maggie II.

My hosts for the weekend, Tom and Rita Royals and their daughter, Kate. While not otherwise occupied during those days I campaigned to get Kate to go to Millsaps College to study English. I won, she went, and had a stellar career there. She became the editor of the Millsaps newspaper and hired my niece, Whitney, when Whitney went to Millsaps two years later. My campaign was based on my love for and belief in Millsaps as a haven for lovers of literature and, also, my newfound idea that we should not send young girls off to school in strange cities where they have no fathers or brothers or cousins to protect them.

The heroine of the entire week was my granddaughter Aurora. No cars were allowed to drive the highways going to New Orleans or the Mississippi or Louisiana coasts. Aurora had been in college for two days when her college was blown away by the hurricane and its attendant tornadoes. She was eighteen years old. Her home and all her possessions were lost and swept out to sea. Her automobile was in a ditch filled with water and would never run again. Her mother was holding up, but was seriously distressed. Her sister, Ellen, at least had a car. It had been in the shop having body work and the shop was above the floodplain.

Aurora had brought both her cats to Jackson, her golden male cat named Ramses and her smaller, smarter female cat named Raszia. As soon as they got to the horse farm, where they spent six nights with my niece and her family, Ramses ran away and has never returned, although he is spotted in the barns by my family. He lives on barn rats, has left civilization and is as large as a wildcat. Aurora had refused to have him spayed so he is living as God and nature intended him to live. Raszia went to Thibodaux, Louisiana, in Aurora's lap.

One week to the day after the hurricane came on land Aurora climbed into the cab of a lime green fourteen wheeler driven by one of her boyfriend's, Raymond Foret's, host of Roman Catholic uncles from the bayou country and was taken down to Thibodaux, Louisiana, where she enrolled in college under the new state doctrine which allowed hurricane victims to enroll in any of the state colleges. She moved into an apartment with two of Raymond's female cousins and started her career as a student at Nicholls State University. She stayed there a year and then transferred to Mississippi State to get a degree in art and business. It is a brilliant degree that teaches artists how to make a business out of their artistic skills.

All of this Aurora arranged on my cellular telephone in two days. While the rest of us were still running around Jackson renting apartments and trying to decide what to do next and waiting to be allowed to go to New Orleans and Ocean Springs to see what remained of everyone's homes, Aurora took herself to Thibodaux, Louisiana, and started college. Credit also belongs to Raymond's large Cajun family, who were kind and generous and took care of her as she made the transition. The uncle who came to get her in the lime green fourteen wheeler is Uncle Joey Carbonell.

There are many stories of young and old people picking up the pieces as quickly as they could and creating new lives out of the debris.

But among my family members eighteen-year-old Aurora Alford Walker was a true leader. I am still awed when I think of how she did all that and convinced us to let her do it.

Testimony of Grandmother Ellen

WHILE EIGHTEEN-YEAR-OLD AURORA WAS TAKING HERSELF DOWN to Thibodaux, Louisiana, to enroll in Nicholls State University, her twenty-year-old sister, Ellen, was packing to go to a farm in southern Denmark to stay with her father and his wife, Catherine, and their three children, William, Camille, and Victoria. Her father has a land surveying company in St. Croix, American Virgin Islands, but lives half the time in Denmark. The farm is in a part of Denmark called Jutland. There are horses to ride and long days to spend getting to know her half-brother and half-sisters.

She stayed two and a half months and made trips to Copenhagen and Paris. In Paris she was met by her mother's college roommate who has sons Ellen's age.

Her mother, Rita, went back to Ocean Springs to finish a job she had running a retail store. She slept several days on a cot in a Red Cross shelter, using a treasured quilt of mine she found in my water-ruined condominium and rescued for me.

The store's owner begged Rita to go down there and salvage what could be saved and clean out the safe. All of that turned out to be difficult to do. There were still shortages of gasoline and bottled water and the highways were torn up everywhere. A close friend of Rita's returned to her unharmed house and Rita went there to stay when she left the Red Cross shelter.

All of this is why no one ever moved into the apartment we had rented. I think I got my money back. I can't remember the details of anything. I had to return to Fayetteville as I am a professor at the

University of Arkansas. Besides our regular students we had a steady influx of students from the devastated areas of Mississippi and Louisiana.

December 29, 2009,
Ocean Springs, Mississippi

BEAUTIFUL CLEAR DAY, 45 DEGREES AND SUNNY. CLEAR SKIES, no wind, warming slowly to 61.

A friend called last night frantic to get some exercise and not have to drive back to Jackson so I took her to the health club and did abdominal exercises while she played in the swimming pool. I love people who are trying to lose weight and become healthy. They have so far to go. They won't give up the foods they think make them happy. The foods don't make them happy. The foods give them momentary pleasure, then they are miserable, thinking, correctly, that they are unattractive, I will teach the ones who really want to learn whatever I can teach them. Setting an example is the only true lesson. Which is why, especially this time of year, I am besieged by members of my family who want to know how to lose weight or how to exercise regularly. Leave your family, I should tell them. Go off and live in a house with no sugar or butter or cookies or sugary drinks.

My friend is only about ten pounds overweight. If she lost the weight she would be happier, more energetic, clearer headed and maybe even mean enough to keep people from using her. If she lost the weight, she might be able to make her children appreciate her sacrifices and sobriety and hard work. I'm pulling for her. She has the idea in her head. Now to put it into practice. I would like to be alone for the next ten days to begin work on a book so I will be in the chips again. So I will have enough money again to never have to count it and to be generous. I love to be generous. My father was generous. I'm in the habit of being generous.

Also I long to understand how to deal with my children and with people I love. I have great love for all my progeny and my brothers and their progeny but I cannot tolerate undisciplined people who drink, take drugs, lie, blame things on other people or allow themselves to be fat and unhealthy. I'd rather have one conversation with the woman emergency room doctor who swims by me at the (embarrassingly silly named) E Fitness and Wellness Center in their seventy-five-foot-long saltwater pool, than spend a day trying to talk to people who are self-destructive. They read books, they talk a good game but they can't put it into play. It takes too long. The game lasts too long. The diet goes on forever, the vigilance is unending.

My friend spent the night. I took her to the health club late in the evening and then insisted she spend the night. I can't let people do that to me when I'm working, but I made an exception for her in honor of the love she cherished on my parents in the last years of their lives.

I went to see my old psychiatrist, Gunther Perdigao, yesterday and said nothing about the death of my parents or the fact that I'm not writing, wasn't writing. I'm writing now. I have to make coffee. If it causes a headache I'll treat it fast and strong. I need to write notes to all the physicians who have treated me in the last few years. Where are my manners that I don't write thank you notes to people who make my life possible?

Gone with the wind like the rest of the beautiful, sensible, Christian culture in which I was fortunate to be raised. My daddy was rich and my momma was good-looking. Even when we weren't rich we lived as though we were. My parents' standards were as unchanging as Greenwich Mean Time.

My father taught us every skill and sport. We learned to use a compass, we built fires without matches. We built lean-tos. We built tents out of blankets. We learned football, basketball, skating, ice skating, walking on stilts he had his men build for us. We had swings in the backyard so high you could swing to heaven if you had the courage. We had it and we didn't call it balls. I'm cleaning up my language. I'm setting standards. My grandfather Gilchrist said he would rather a son of his be dead than be a drunk. Anyone who drinks or gets really fat is dead to me. No more compromising.

I was in a fabulous mood when I left Gunther yesterday. I don't understand why I felt so good. Perhaps it is the good, loving care he nourished on me when I really needed it, trapped in a sexless marriage with a darling man who was too short for me to love.

I married the father of my children to make love to him. I married James Nelson Bloodworth for his books and newspapers and because he was a judge. He couldn't make me come. He was embarrassed by sex. Then I married Freddy Kullman for his money and his wealthy and powerful Jewish family and to get my children out of the terrible Rankin County school Daddy had built for them. Marshall and Garth both wish they had stayed there with my brilliant, interesting, charismatic, alpha alpha male father and brothers.

Marshall has built a farm in Denmark, in Jutland, that is a replica of the one I made him leave in Rankin County. Also, my father was right about the people who teach in public schools and colleges. Now that I am a professor I see all around me every day the taxpayers' money being squandered on ridiculous politically correct hires and classes.

I will see Gunther again on Thursday. Perhaps I will have an epiphany. Perhaps not. It is worth a try. Worrying about the lives of my grown children is a waste of energy. Worrying over my teaching job is equally useless.

I am a writer. People love to read what I write. Now to make it something I can publish without cheating on what I really think.

Ode to New Orleans

THIS IS A PERSONAL ESSAY. I DO NOT PRETEND TO SPEAK FOR ALL the people of New Orleans, many of whom live lives that are very different from mine. I have visited New Orleans for long periods of time ever since I was a child, and I lived there from 1967 to 1977. Since I moved away I have come back to visit many times each year and own a condominium ninety miles away in Ocean Springs, Mississippi, which was flooded by the storm surge from Hurricane Katrina. Many people I love live in New Orleans. My youngest son lives there, as does my oldest grandson and five of my granddaughters. The fate of the city is part of my fate.

Most of my family left before the storm came, but they left at the last minute, taking nothing with them but a few clothes, although a farsighted daughter-in-law did spend an hour collecting portraits of her parents and grandparents. She is an only child and cherishes such things more than most of us do. Or else she was just more prescient.

For as long as I have been visiting or living in New Orleans the natives, black and white, rich and poor, highly educated and barely educated, have refused to leave the city when there were hurricane warnings. They have drunken parties and fill their bathtubs with water and meet at crowded grocery stores to buy flashlight batteries and canned food and talk about hurricanes they have "weathered" and where the mayor is "riding it out" and how much they hope the pumping stations will keep working, although no one I knew had ever been to see a pumping station or understood how they worked. Let the good times roll.

Cities are like families, the inhabitants have common ways of being. In New Orleans riding out hurricanes is how you tell the natives from the *arrivistes* from less cosmopolitan places like Alabama and Mississippi.

I am from Mississippi so I always heeded the hurricane warnings. I would throw my children into my old Rambler station wagon and drive up to Jackson to visit my father and mother. "Tornadoes will follow you to Jackson," everyone always yelled after me. "Nothing's going to happen here. It never does."

No one—except climatologists and weather forecasters, who New Orleanians are practiced at ignoring—ever dreamed a category five hurricane would actually come ashore and bring a flood in its wake. No one believed the canal levees would break and take back land New Orleanians jokingly brag about as being below sea level, as if they are above the laws of gravity and motion and such concerns as sea levels.

New Orleanians are Roman Catholics and Orthodox and Reform Jews, they are French and Spanish and have exotic names like Rafael and Gunther and Thibodaux and Rosaleigh. They are African and voodoo and have built protestant churches with choirs that rival the Mormon Tabernacle. They have survived yellow fever and malaria in the 1800s and found ways to kill the mosquitoes and control the Mississippi River with levees so high and wide you can drive cars on top of them.

"There are the levees and the pumping stations to protect us," they used to tell me. "Hurricanes never hit New Orleans. (Well, there was Betsy.) They always turn back to the east before they make landfall. The city will be all right. Besides, we can't leave. We have to stay and take care of the house, the pets, the store. Momma doesn't want to leave."

So when large numbers of men and women, most of whom were educated and could read and had working vehicles and telephones and could call someone to take them out of town, elected not to leave New Orleans after their mayor gave them a mandatory evacuation order, I was not surprised.

I know the place and the people.

What happened next was both dazzling and embarrassing. The dazzling part was the way thousands of men and women risked their own health and safety to come to the aid of the people who were stranded when the levees failed—the doctors and nurses of Tulane Medical Center and Charity Hospital who worked without electricity, food, or sleep to save patients; courageous individuals who brought in boats and launched personal rescue operations in fetid water; and my favorite student in Fayetteville, Arkansas, who took a three-week leave of absence to go to New Orleans with her helicopter rescue unit.

The embarrassing part was when people started blaming the disaster on hard-working people like Mayor Ray Nagin and Governor Kathleen Blanco. Hurricanes are caused by weather patterns on the oceans. They might as well have blamed the oceans, or the coast of Africa where the storms begin, or the islands in the Caribbean that didn't take the blow before it swept into the Gulf of Mexico.

New Orleanians suffered a great loss, and there is much remorse and guilt for not being prescient. But that is how it always is with the human race in times of disaster. The cerebral cortex is only a hundred thousand years old. We aren't yet smart enough to heed warnings and stop blaming other people when we really are mad at ourselves.

I hope the next time there is a mandatory evacuation order more people will leave the city, but if there are several false alarms, this laudable behavior will wear thin. The climate in New Orleans is not good for sustained logical thinking. The early mornings are tropical and fragrant, full of promise, the best coffee in the world, and beautiful people wearing soft white clothing and sandals. No wonder everyone wants to return.

Late in May of 2006, I visited the city for five days and found myself caught up in the fun and beauty of the place. Only nine months after that terrible disaster and already people are starting to bloom like the azaleas and cape jasmine and honeysuckle that perfume the air. There is much talk everywhere about Katrina cottages and lawsuits against insurance companies and being in limbo about whether to rebuild.

The tools needed to build a new New Orleans are patience, discipline, gratefulness, concentration, dedication, and imagination. The same tools we learn in yoga. Anger, fear, and greed are the enemies of getting anything done. Of course all the good will and work in the world won't help if another huge storm hits the city before the levees are strengthened and rebuilt. A stalled front after a storm would cause worse flooding than Katrina did. So much depends on the weather, but this is life on planet earth. We have always been subject to the will of the heavens although some of us have been lucky to live in a time and place where we could forget that for a while.

I've decided that the best thing to do about New Orleans with its hurricanes and floods and improbability is to sit in zazen and be glad the place is there and that I have been privileged to know it. I'm going to hang new prayer flags in my cherry trees in honor of the city of New Orleans and the courage and beauty of its many-colored people.

If I go back to worrying about the always uncertain future and the precariousness of human life, I will read *The Storm* by Ivor van Heerden, deputy director of the Louisiana State University Hurricane Center. Van Heerden says if we don't get to work and construct state-of-the-art levees and wetlands protection, water will eventually take back all the land to Interstate 10, which would be the end of New Orleans as we know it.

When I get through meditating and putting up prayer flags, I'd better start writing and calling my congressmen and remind them they have work to do.

Casting a Cold Eye

I HAVE A MIDWESTERN HEART AND THE COLD EYE OF AN INVES-
tigative reporter. A lot of the mystery and romance of New Orleans
is about alcohol. Let's say fifty percent is about drinking and the rest
is about beautiful restaurants and cocktail parties and white-coated
waiters and wonderful, exotic, French food and wines. It is about
the huge, beautiful mansions built by slaves or people who were
little better than slaves. Irish stonemasons, Italian carpenters, and
lately, British painters, Mexican roofers. The roofers swoop in in
the early morning. There will be a driver who speaks English and a
pickup truck full of sweet-hearted, hardworking men playing wonderful music on cheap radios. Not a green card among them; the
owners of the houses being painted know and laugh about it. Cast
a blind eye is the mantra when keeping the mansions in shape with
Hondurans, Mexicans, Nicaraguans, and African Americans who
have not agreed to learn to speak the sort of English that will get
them a desk job.

The sweet smell of marijuana floats among the toxic fumes of
paint and mold-killing Kilz and the chemicals being sprayed on the
lice and rodents and roaches that live in those old mansions no matter how much poison you use to make them go next door and propa-
gate. Not to even mention Formosan termites and regular old Louisiana termites.

All will be well. The Mardi Gras costumes are safe in chemically
sealed plastic bags. The queens and kings and ladies-in-waiting and
pages take off their costumes when the balls are over and they are

whisked away to be sealed up for posterity in special cedar closets no roach dare enter.

Things that I took for granted the ten years I tried to live in New Orleans but which now annoy me include waiters who expect huge tips and keep on being haughty even after you turn over the tribute, salaried men at the airport who literally won't touch your luggage until you hand them five- or ten-dollar bills. I like tipping people but I don't like to feel as though my luggage will be stolen if I don't hand over a twenty-dollar bill. You aren't supposed to have to tip salaried employees of airlines to check in your luggage at the curb. I have flown all over the world and New Orleans is the pirate city of airline employees.

What else annoys me about New Orleans? Taxi drivers from hell, many of whom don't speak English, won't turn off the radio or turn on the air conditioning, and expect even bigger tips than their buddies at the airport.

I hate parallel parking on narrow crowded streets with potholes and the fact that parking tickets are one of the major sources of funding for the city. When I was there in the spring semester of 2005, to have a wonderful time and be feted at Tulane University and hold a chair in the humanities and another at the Women's Center of Newcomb College, it seemed to me that a third of the police force was engaged in parking scams. I was fined fifty dollars for parking in the wrong direction in front of my rented house. No warning. The first night I slept in the house I parked my car in front of it and when I got up at seven the next morning there was a ticket. This after having spent an entire afternoon the day before driving out to City Park to pay seventy-five dollars for a permit and sticker to park in front of my house. Tulane sent one of their office staff with me to make sure I had a personal check. The office where the permits are granted does not accept cash or credit cards. It is manned by three obese women who file their nails and talk on cellular telephones while the roomful of applicants sit politely on hard chairs holding little numbers they are given as they enter. Outside the office a morbidly obese police officer stands guard. This man is so fat it is unbelievable. How they made a policeman's uniform to fit him is another amazing question. Around the corner two more obese but still basically human-looking policemen sit on a bench earning their paychecks by some mysterious thinking process. I was told by the Tulane employee that all of these people were political appointees, part of the bottomless corruption of the city government. My uncle was the editor of the *Times-Picayune*, the main newspaper of New Orleans. In his time the city was run by the southern Mafia and the office of mayor was handed down, as it is now, by a family of politically astute pirates.

Before the hurricane and after the hurricane the same hierarchy holds sway. The corruption and lack of real jobs never change. There are jobs on the port, jobs in the tourist industry, jobs selling dope, lawyers and physicians and medical personnel, three universities, yard work, interior decorators and antique dealers and small shops where wealthy people buy expensive clothes for themselves and their dogs and their children, coffee shops and that's about it, except temporary government jobs teaching the arts to African American students. Plus the Saints games and the struggling symphony orchestra.

The government pours money into New Orleans. It has poured money into New Orleans for a hundred years but nothing much ever changes.

There are wonderful people in the city, rich and poor, white and cocoa colored and black and light brown and dark brown, Caucasian, African American, Vietnamese, and a constantly changing mix of Mexicans and Central and South Americans and French and Belgians and Englishmen and -women who specialize in haughtily looking down their English noses at everyone's accents.

It's a constantly changing mix of nations and creeds and costumes and sights. Fifty-year-old white women running in and out of Langenstein's in their tennis dresses, every man and woman a law unto themselves where fashion and manners is concerned. You can be knocked off the sidewalk by an African bicycle rider and helped into the car by a stranger in the same block.

~ ~ ~

I hope the federal government keeps on pouring money into this poor but attractive relative of a city. I hope the music never stops and the movie stars keep coming in and buying up all the good houses in the lower garden district.

I wish we could find a way to rebuild the city that did not depend on handouts and people coming there to get drunk and throw trash down on the streets. I really dislike Mardi Gras. It used to be a beautiful, funny, local celebration with grown men being silly enough to pretend they were kings and people seeing through the absurdity and buying into it at the same time.

Now it is a big, overgrown, two-week-long, drunken bacchanal with people coming in from all over the world to get drunk and throw things down on the streets and the next morning big trucks full of poor people coming along behind them to pick up the mess. The trucks burn lots of petrol we buy from the Middle East where the best sons of the poor people go to fight (and sometimes die) because they can't find a decent job doing anything else.

And so on.

There are times in the early mornings when I go out to run in Audubon Park and the beauty and soft, moisture-laden air and the huge old oak trees are so wonderful I can't help but love New Orleans.

I hear the bells from Loyola University and see the tall handsome buildings of Tulane University and I think of my physician uncles and great-uncles who were educated there and my doctor grandson and artist granddaughters who recently graduated there. I think of the writing class I once took from a poet at Tulane and the fun of hearing poetry readings in the lovely chapel. I remember the honors they gave me only five years ago and the dinner parties and seventieth birthday party they had for me with three wonderful cakes. I remember when we plastered the campus with signs and gave away buttons saying A SOUND MIND IN A SOUND BODY, both in English and in Latin.

I remember the Thursday afternoon class I taught and how, almost to a man and woman, the students wrote about the dangers and problems getting drunk had caused them or their friends. One story ended in a death, as drunken stories often do.

These were beautiful, upper-middle-class children, some the children of professors and teachers, who had been sent to Tulane to learn to have sound minds in sound bodies, but they had been taught to get drunk at the same time. On the one hand, geology and history and philosophy and literature and biology and geometry and higher math and chemistry and biochemistry and astrophysics and plain physics and architecture and music and art. On the other hand getting drunk at parties and in the French Quarter and at the lake and in automobiles and in bars, bars, bars.

It made me cry to read their stories. I read the same stories at the University of Arkansas but they aren't this sad and every student doesn't write them. This was a hand-picked class of the best students at the university. The homecoming queen wrote about her sadness that the beautiful young man she loved was ruining his life with alcohol and she was helpless to save him.

Another student was spending his spare time trying to get his roommate to stop driving when he was drunk and stoned.

I hope the beautiful and good parts of the city can be rebuilt and that industries will come that will give the citizens of New Orleans something to do that adds to the store of goodness in the world.

I want drunkenness and drugs and prostitution and pornography and bad art to be left in the past, drowned beneath the flood. The pitiful artists who sell their ugly paintings to the tourists. The smelly bars with their Tennessee Williams imitators and all of that. You can have it. I quit drinking thirty-five years ago. I don't like it anymore. I see no reason to tolerate it and let it ruin our lives and the lives of our children.

January 1, 2010

WONDERFUL DAY YESTERDAY IN A SUNNY WARM NEW ORLEANS.
I spent an hour with Gunther Perdigao. Gunther. What an amazing thing the human mind really is. Those deep memories of all the hours I spent with him when I was a confused, unfulfilled thirty-four- and thirty-five- and thirty-six- and thirty-seven-year-old. The behaviorist Chet Scrignar had taught me to stop drinking, a Gargantuan task and worthy of his brilliant, powerful mind and personality. Then Gunther spent four afternoons a week listening to me weep years of frustration and confusion on his couch. All this time I was writing poetry, writing it fiercely, praising the beautiful world in which I was confused and suffering, praising all creation while trying desperately to figure out how to become a person I could bear to be.

Just remember that you're standing on a planet that's evolving
And revolving at nine hundred miles an hour,
That's orbiting at nineteen miles a second, so it's reckoned,
A sun that is the source of all our power.
The sun and you and me and all the stars that we can see
Are moving at a million miles a day
In an outer spiral arm, at forty thousand miles an hour,
Of the galaxy we call the 'Milky Way'.
Our galaxy itself contains a hundred billion stars.
It's a hundred thousand light years side to side.
It bulges in the middle, sixteen thousand light years thick,
But out by us, it's just three thousand light years wide.

We're thirty thousand light years from galactic central point.
We go 'round every two hundred million years,
And our galaxy is only one of millions of billions
In this amazing and expanding universe.

The universe itself keeps on expanding and expanding
In all of the directions it can whizz
As fast as it can go, at the speed of light, you know,
Twelve million miles a minute, and that's the fastest speed there is.
So remember, when you're feeling very small and insecure,
How amazingly unlikely is your birth,
And pray that there's intelligent life somewhere up in space,
'Cause there's bugger all down here on Earth.

Gunther and I talked about my youngest son, Pierre, for an hour that seemed like two minutes.

December 29, 2009,
Ocean Springs, Mississippi
The Mystery of Psychotherapy
The Mystery of Transference
The Hardwired Banks of the River Memory

―――――――――――――――― ⦿ ――――――――――――――――

ONE OF THE SADDEST THINGS ABOUT DEATH IS THAT IT ERASES the rivers of memory, the vast store of faces, places, events, time, weather, excitement, games, imagination, ideas, love.

I am on the Mississippi coast for five weeks over the Christmas holidays. Which means I take off the rational hats I wear as writer and teacher in the college town of Fayetteville, Arkansas, and put on the kinder, sillier face more suited to a grandmother and great-grandmother.

I have three sons and my sometimes troubled attempts to tell them what to do continue, no matter how hard I try to remember that it is an impossible task, not to mention unworthy of a seventy-five-year-old woman who should be satisfied with unconditional love.

"For they live in the house of the future, which you cannot visit, not even in your dreams."

Here they are, visiting India, having many wonderful children, surveying swamps and catching viral diseases like malaria and dengue fever. Getting well in record time. Sailing two-hundred-foot-long boats from Louisiana to Brazil, fighting custody battles with an ex-wife and her terrible mother, loving their wives, loving their children, laughing, fishing, hunting, driving pickup trucks, patting me on the head.

I am constantly afraid something bad will happen to them if they don't live as carefully as I do. I should have a sign in my house that says, "No smoking, no drinking, no wild ideas, no motorcycles or fast cars or flying airplanes or piloting large boats across the equator and around the Cape of Good Horn, no being like my brothers or your forefathers.

"All I'm really saying is, keep breathing. I love you, your lives dazzle me. I need everyone to stay alive until I can learn to do this unconditional love thing. Love, your mother."

I might as well have a sign. I've been so judgmental for so many years they all know never to smoke or drink in front of me. They like to bring the children to see me. I adore little children. At least they pretend to listen to me even if the ones with big brains give me that look when I start telling them not to climb high things at the park. They keep on climbing. "I won't fall," even the four-year-old tells me. And keeps on climbing.

Because I am sometimes bored when I stay at my little house on the coast waiting for them to bring the children to see me, I thought up calling my old psychotherapist and asking him if I could have a few appointments to talk about mothering grown children.

He agreed and the next morning I drove the ninety miles from Ocean Springs to New Orleans and spent an hour talking nonstop about the huge cast of characters I have acquired since this dear man helped me find myself. It was in his office that I cried my tears and found the courage to become a writer and left my sweet, wealthy husband and went to Fayetteville, Arkansas, to live the life I had always meant to live. I didn't abandon my children. They had already abandoned me by taking drugs and not giving a damn about a thing but the madness of the nineteen seventies.

"If they won't use the genes, then I'll use them," I had told this psychotherapist, whose name is Gunther and whom I had been seeing four days a week for several years.

I became a writer. I fulfilled my dreams. I made my way in the world alone. I made a good living and used most of the money to help my now somewhat repentant sons get educations and become useful members of society.

All of that was so long ago, so many long years ago, so many wives and girlfriends and children ago, so many books that I wrote and published, so many lectures around the United States and in Europe, so many fine adventures I was given and so many fans I acquired and honors I received.

But at the core of my being are these three sons and their progeny, these gene-bearers, these wonderful little boys and girls.

So mysterious, all of this. None of it more mysterious than the three afternoons I just spent sitting in the office of my old psychotherapist and delving deep into all this history and all the old fears and guilt. I bury fear. I John Wayne fear. "That will be the day," I think, if I dream of dying or of losing any battle other than the endless one I wage to control my uncontrollable sons.

Always, since the very first day I was alone in a room with H. Gunther Perdigao, M.D., I have been able to let the fears and rage show their ugly faces, and, in his presence, with him listening, I beat them down, I right hook and left hook and kill shot them. I refuse to be fearful of anything human, except, of course, disease and disability. So let me put it this way, I refuse to fear anything, only excepting mortality and its causes.

It's a battle and I'm waging it as hard as I can. Exercise, careful diet, constant vigilance, flu shots, pneumonia shots, detox diets, Dr. Andrew Weil's vitamins and anti-aging Juvenon, and so much else. I'm armed and dangerous when it comes to aging. I'm ready to go the distance with preventing disease.

All of these ideas and musings, these memories and questionings, these vibrantly alive doings and dreams, this wild, vibrant life I've led, all came rushing out as I talked to Gunther again after all these years. I talked without ceasing for almost an hour each time I saw him and, when he told me it was time to stop, I kept on talking as I said goodbye and left the room and went out the door onto the street. I could not stop at his command. I had to put a coda on what I had been saying, to reassure him, although he had not asked to be reassured, that my leaving was all right, that I knew psychotherapy is long, its goals are unformed and unknown until the unconscious mind forces an end, or answers a question, and you seem to know what it was you were doing, and that there is an answer, of sorts, and a way is prepared before you to proceed with your life in a better, clearer way.

It is so difficult to tell anyone who wasn't in the room what it was that happened there or why it seems to be important.

When I was in psychotherapy with Gunther I found out what my strengths were, I remembered my great talent as a writer, I wrote my heart out and talked my heart out and then I left a very nice, very wealthy man. Although I loved and honored him, I could not fulfill my work as a writer until I was alone, with no one looking over my shoulder or being afraid of what I was writing.

"He is called a poet, not he who writeth in measure only, but he who formeth and fayneth a fable and writes things like the truth."

On the third afternoon I spent with Gunther something happened that must be noted. There were physical reasons for what happened. I had driven three hours that morning in a rickety little Honda I bought to keep on the coast. It was freezing cold. I had not eaten much and probably hadn't drunk enough water.

But that is not the reason that when I stood up from Gunther's chair I was dizzy. I overcame it and told him goodbye, imagining that it was temporary or a low blood sugar problem from not eating. When I began to drive down the crooked, crowded streets of uptown New Orleans I was still dizzy but in control. I went to the Whole Foods Market on Magazine Street and bought food and ate it. Then, because they didn't have aspirin for sale, I went to Langenstein's Grocery Store and bought a bottle of water and a bottle of aspirins and took one in case I was having a stroke. I didn't think I was having a stroke. I was just covering my bases.

It was cold and grey outside, deep cloud cover all the way to Canada, freezing cold for New Orleans. I could have called my grandson, who is a fourth-year medical student at Tulane. I could have called my son Pierre, or his wife, or my ex-daughter-in-law, or my granddaughters or my cousins. I could have gone to the emergency room at Touro Infirmary, but I'd had enough doctors for one day.

I drove home to Ocean Springs, very, very carefully, watching closely to see if I became more dizzy or in any way unable to drive.

I stopped three times on the way home. When I would get out of the car and stand up the dizziness would return but I could walk in a straight line.

At the Mississippi State Rest Area near the state line I took a second aspirin after talking to some strangers about whether it was safe to take two full-strength aspirins.

When I finally got home I became sicker. I called my grandson and a cranial masseuse and read about dizziness in the Mayo Medical Dictionary. We all decided it was an inner ear problem from swimming although I had no ear symptoms or pain.

I took a Zyrtec and a Mucinex in case the dizziness was caused by allergies. Then I went upstairs and lay down on my bed to pull on my ears as recommended by the cranial masseur and the Mayo Medical Dictionary.

As soon as I lay down the room began to spin. Vertigo, just as I had suspected. Then I got up and went to the toilet and threw up the entire contents of my stomach. I felt better although I was in pain in all my limbs, not excruciating but enough to keep me from moving.

In awhile I fell asleep and slept eleven or twelve hours, just waking occasionally to urinate and drink more water.

In the morning I felt shaky but much better. I went to the cranial masseur and he worked on my head for two hours and I was better. Now it is a day later and I'm still shaky and unsure of myself.

It's freezing outside. Record-breaking cold for the Mississippi coast. I will read and write all day and ponder this mystery. I purged after I talked to Gunther. This is a fact that will not go away. I came to him thirty years ago after a brain concussion caused by drinking and falling down a flight of stairs. That was the last drink I ever had except for a couple of times. When I got drunk, I went back to Antabuse for months afterwards. I will not drink and be a drunk. It is never going to happen to me again.

Drinking is my enemy and the people from whom I am descended. I hate it. I fight it in my students, in my progeny, anywhere I am in contact with its destructive power.

While Talking to Gunther Perdigao
on January 3, 2010

I WAS TALKING NONSTOP, FREE ASSOCIATING LIKE MAD.
Memory is so amazing, so vital and clear and all it is is chemistry. Or magic. I think it is magic after the three hours I just spent with Gunther. I hope to God I don't lose my memory before I die. I don't mind dying, as long as I do it my way. I will do it my way. I have a long time to screw my courage to that sticking point, but I will stick it. I think. I hope.

Great doors were opened for me by becoming a writer and the fame it gave me whether I wanted fame or not. I didn't like it. Its pleasures are not worth having your life opened to all sorts of people you wouldn't ordinarily choose as friends.

One never-to-be-forgotten thrill was getting to fly in the cockpit of the British Airlines Concorde, when the Concorde was new. I was sitting next to the president of Lloyd's of London, the company which insures the British Airlines planes. We talked for awhile. I told him I was going to London to meet my British publishers at Faber and Faber. I told him I had never been to the British Isles although my ancestry was English and Scots.

"We are landing at dawn British time," he said. "Would you like to sit in the cockpit so you can see the British Isles from the air?"

"Would I like to sit in the cockpit of the Concorde? Good lord, you must be kidding."

Thirty minutes before landing a steward came down the aisle and took me to the cockpit and I sat in the fourth officer's chair behind the pilot. The cockpit was like a small room, almost square. From my seat I could see out the wide windows of the plane and when the British Isles came into view they were spread out before me like a beautiful living map.

"Thank you so much for letting me be here," I told the three officers in the other seats. "I promise not to touch anything."

"It would be better if none of us touched anything," the pilot said. He was laughing. "Computers land this aircraft."

We all laughed then and watched as the home of my ancestors was lit by the rising sun.

February 13, 2010

A DEEP WINTER FOG AT SIX-THIRTY IN THE MORNING. I CAN'T even see my neighbors' lights. Very beautiful, and warm enough to walk outside in a bathrobe for the first time in weeks. The coldest winter in decades all over the United States. It even snowed in Ocean Springs, Mississippi, two days ago. It covered the Dallas airport in snow. I ran into Carolyn Walton at the health club yesterday morning. She and Nick are going to south Texas for two weeks.

The day before my birthday I'm going to Ocean Springs to build a huge cake covered with candles and let my grandchildren and sons help me blow it out. What fun. Then, if the weather is good, we will build a bonfire on the beach and watch it burn. We have to clean it up afterwards, which isn't as much fun, but so what? That's what tall strong grandchildren are for.

I made coffee and went back outside at six-forty-five and there was light in the sky. Not as beautiful as it was right before sunrise but still beautiful. The fog means that warm air is moving in from the coast. Hallelujah. I don't fear cold and winter, I just hate it.

It's nearing my birthday, the time when the days start seeming longer and the winter seems bearable. As always I wish I had planted bulbs in the fall, but I never do. It would make me too mad when the squirrels and rabbits ate them, as they would surely do.

Mother, Father, Ancestors: The People Who Made Me

Wyoming, 1976

———⟨⟩———

MY FATHER TOOK ONE VACATION IN HIS LONG HARD-WORKING life. He was gone two years, high in the mountains of Wyoming, riding the snow-covered roads in a covered pickup truck, or on horses, and finally, coming down the slopes on skis. My mother was with him for awhile but she was a southern lady and could not figure out how to live in cold and snow. Also, she did not share my father's vision of a new land opening before them where they could bring their children and grandchildren and save them from the madness that was infesting the cities and small towns of the American South.

"They're not going to come out here and live and run dry cleaning establishments," she told him. "Just because they come out here and hunt and drive around with you doesn't mean they are going to tear up their lives and come live here."

"We'll start again, Bodie. Just like our great-grandfathers did. I'll buy Bob a small bank to run. At Christmas I'm going to bring them all out to learn to ski. You'll see. They'll love it. How could they resist?"

"It's too cold," she kept saying. "I can't even go outside. I'm too old for this, Dooley. I have followed you around all your life and finally I'm back in Mississippi with my friends and my family and I'm going to stay there."

"Wait until after Christmas. Wait until I get them on the slopes."

So she agreed to wait. He had bought her a beautiful modern home with six bedrooms and sheds for the ski equipment and a

49

heated garage but she was having a hard time finding any help. The big monosyllabic German women he found for her barely dusted and they were too big to get under the beds. She longed for her old maids, small, elegant black women who shared her vision of how to set a table or make up a bed or answer the phone or let visitors in. Not that they had many visitors in Casper, Wyoming, although her sons did fly in without notice and spend the night now and then.

After six months, especially after all the chaos of the skiing trip at Christmas, she gave up and went home to live in New Orleans near me and her sisters, Margaret and Roberta.

Two months later, in the spring, Daddy went to Mexico and got a divorce and married the other grandmother of his six grand-daughters. Her name was Lucy Benedict and she had been in love with him since the day she met him. She came right out and Daddy moved to Buffalo, Wyoming, and bought a ranch. It had been his first choice all along but he thought Mother could tolerate the larger town of Casper better.

That marriage lasted two years, what Daddy called his vacation, then Lucy went back home to Nashville with five hundred thousand dollars and Daddy went down to New Orleans with his hat in his hand and begged Mother to forgive him and help him with his plan to move back to Jackson near the grandchildren and save them from the chaos of the 1970s. "Kathleen is running around with a black man," he said, with tears in his eyes. "We have to go back to Jackson and do something with those girls."

Mother wavered for awhile, consulting with her sisters and with me. She had moved to New Orleans and was living around the corner from me in an elegant duplex on Henry Clay Avenue. She was going to Mardi Gras balls with my Uncle George and Aunt Margaret and being squired around town by attractive men her age, including an old beau from her glory days at Ole Miss. Also she was spending long days with her younger sister, Roberta, who was trying to recover from the death of her oldest son in a drunk driving accident in Jackson just before my parents moved to Wyoming from the farm in Rankin County. Neither my cousin Chris or his girlfriend had been drinking. A Jackson matron barreled around a corner of Fortification and High streets, ignored a red light and hit them head on.

St. Vincent's Hospital called my parents at two in the morning and they went to the hospital to watch Charles Christian Klienschmidt die. Within hours my Aunt Roberta and Uncle Charlie and their fraternal twins, Nell and Ken, and half the congregation of Saint Paul's Episcopal Church of Metairie, Louisiana, were in Jackson staying on my parents' eighty-acre farm or in the area and walking around my mother's parlors trying to think of something comforting to say.

My father asked me to take the twelve-year-old twins off to distract them for awhile. I had a new white Chevrolet Camaro he had given me as a reward for the straight A's I was making at Millsaps in an attempt to complete the education I had interrupted to have three sons. On old Highway 90 I had noticed a new automatic car washing machine. You drove into the machine and it washed the car with you sitting in it. I'd been wanting to try it, so as soon as I got Ken and Nell in the car we drove around the farm for awhile and then I took them to try out the car washing machine.

It was a terrifying adventure but they both enjoyed it, Ken sitting in the front seat with me and Nell staunchly sitting in the back with her hands folded in her lap. If either of them were frightened they didn't let it show.

I wish I could remember what I talked to them about. I'm pretty sure I told them about going to see Chris the week before to talk about what classes he should sign up for for the spring semester. He had called me, probably at Aunt Roberta's urging, and I had driven right over to see if I could help.

He was tall and blond and blue-eyed and serious. A serious young man with a lovely shy smile. He still had a few pimples, which he was covering with a colored paste young people used back then. My young husband, the father of my children, had suffered pimples until he was twenty-four so I was sympathetic to Chris's plight and full of advice. "That makeup stuff looks good," I think I said.

"Please don't worry about a few pimples. It's only one or two. My husband, Marshall, had lots more than that and I fell madly in love with him and had three children. You are so tall a girl can't even see them."

I had picked him up behind his dormitory on a narrow campus street. When I got there he was standing waiting for me, looking so much like the boy his age I had married not many years before, tall, straight, serious, beautifully dressed in khaki pants and a light blue oxford cloth shirt, a narrow, handsome belt, and a patterned tie.

"I have a girlfriend," he told me. "You'll meet her. I'm going to bring her out to the farm to meet Aunt Bodie and Uncle Dooley. She's from the delta. She's a Chi Omega like Momma and Aunt Bodie and Cousin Nell and you. She's a year older than I am, but we don't care. Well, not a whole year. Just a year ahead in school because she started when she was five. Her name is Janet Harbison. She says I should go S.A.E. because they don't drink as much as the Phi Delts and the Kappa Sigs. I don't know. I'm more interested in signing up for classes next semester."

"Take Dr. Boyd's Shakespeare class. If you get worried about reading it, call me up and I'll come over and read it to you and tell you about it. You have to know Shakespeare to be an educated person, Chris. You can't just take any old thing. We are from generations of Greek and Latin scholars. You're here to become an educated gentleman. Really, promise me you'll take it."

"I will. I have to choose the classes tomorrow."

"Go this afternoon before it fills up. Dr. Boyd's the best teacher in the English Department. He's the one who let me be in Eudora Welty's class at the last minute."

"Okay, I will. Momma told me to talk to you. I like your new car. It's really pretty."

"Daddy gave it to me for making A's in science and math. Did you know I'm writing a play for New Stage Theatre about Miss Welty's stories? Well, it's made out of her stories. All I'm doing is dramatizing them."

"Janet told me about that. She read it in the newspaper. She wants to meet you, Cousin Ellen. She really does."

"Let's go over to the Union and get something to eat. Are you hungry?"

"I'm hungry all the time. I'm on a football team for the S.A.E.'s. I guess that's the one I'll join. I don't want to hurt anyone's feelings."

"You're lucky. When I was at Vanderbilt I didn't get bids to the three best sororities. I'd never even heard of any of them. All I knew about was Chi Omega. I got my feelings hurt so bad when I didn't get bids to them. I still can't understand it, but Momma says it's because I didn't have recommendations to them. I don't think so. I think it's because I gained ten pounds the first two months I was at Vandy. I was homesick and I didn't know people up there and I just started eating my head off.

"I've lost it now but when I look at photographs of that fall I know why they didn't give me bids. I thought because I was so smart and made good grades and published poetry and wrote for the newspaper they would all like me like everyone always has." I think we laughed at that. I want to think we did.

"Do you get lonely here at Millsaps? Are there other people from New Orleans here, other boys?"

"Not many. Not anyone I know. But some of our cousins from the delta and sons of Momma's friends from Ole Miss are here."

I had stopped the car and he jumped out and came across and held the door open for me and we walked together across the campus, kicking the fall leaves and being glad we were cousins. He was so nice, so special.

Telling the story to Ken and Nell, I almost started crying, but the water and the huge brushes were beating on the car so hard it made me stop.

Ken was leaned all the way into the windshield watching the machine. Nell was sitting quietly in the back.

We drove out of the drive-through car wash and went back to the farm and I took them out to my cottage and let them watch the new television set while I went inside to talk to the mourners. I kept going up to Uncle Charlie and Aunt Roberta and trying to think of something to say. I just said anything I could think up, but none of it helped them or me.

A car arrived at the front door and Daddy went outside and brought Chris's girlfriend, Janet, into the house with her mother and her father. She sat near Aunt Roberta all afternoon while my mother talked to her mother.

The next day we all drove down to the delta to my grandparents' plantation and all our relatives came there and our Aunt Zell and Uncle Floyd fed everyone and talked to them and we spent the night at Hopedale, where Aunt Roberta had lived every day of her life, mostly being happy and cared for and loved.

Now she was here to bury a child. The worst thing that can happen to a human being is to bury a child. It had already happened to my Aunt Margaret and Uncle George and I don't think they ever recovered from it. Now it was Aunt Roberta and Uncle Charlie's turn.

Two months before we had all been in the same place burying my grandmother, Nell Biggs Alford, "Dan-Dan." At nine in the morning the next day we went to the Episcopal Church in Rolling Fork and had the same service for Chris we had had for Dan-Dan. Except there were many young men and women in the church, cousins and S.A.E.'s and Chi Omegas from Millsaps College.

Then we drove out in the country to the ruins of the beautiful brick Episcopal Church my ancestors had built in the 1880s and buried Chris beside my grandmother and grandfather and my great-grandmother and great-grandfather and the twins Dan-Dan lost at birth, and my cousin Floyd who was just my age and had been my playmate for eight years until he died from anesthesia in Touro Infirmary while having a small operation to straighten a broken index finger on his left hand.

It was a beautiful clear day with soft cirrus clouds turning the golden sunlight into pink and mauve and blue and violet and soft yellows. All those graves, the one where only the ashes of my great-grandfather were buried because he died of yellow fever and they had to burn the body on the levee because my Uncle Robert was afraid it would spread the disease. Uncle Robert was buried here too. Robert Finley, M.D., for whom Aunt Roberta was named because he had delivered her when she was born right after Dan-Dan lost the twins.

Our living twins were beautiful and strong. Aunt Roberta had carried them nine months and they had weighed eight and nine pounds, respectively. I can't remember which one came first or which one was the biggest although I was there, at the hospital with my mother and my brother. They were so cute and as soon as they got back to her house from the hospital Aunt Roberta put them in the same bed because she and Uncle Charlie decided they might be lonely for each other in separate beds.

It was out on the lake front, in Aunt Roberta's living room, drinking coffee from my great-grandmother's demitasse cups, that my mother decided to give my father another chance. Aunt Margaret was still objecting but Aunt Roberta pled my father's case and my mother forgave him. She punished him later by not letting him celebrate their fiftieth wedding anniversary which was a few years later.

I had already told Mother to go back to him. I hated to have her leave New Orleans because she was very useful to me as a babysitter for my youngest son, Pierre, but down in my heart I always took my father's side in everything. So what if he had married my older brother's mother-in-law for two years? He only did it because Momma refused to live in Wyoming because the women were so ugly and fat and it was so cold she could hardly stand to go to the grocery store.

After Mother said yes to Daddy we had to plan a second wedding for my parents. They were seventy-one years old and Mother wanted to be married in the cathedral on Saint Charles Avenue by the bishop of Louisiana. She had been the director of music for the bishop for two years while Daddy was in Wyoming having articles written about him in magazines for learning to ski when he was seventy years old.

~ ~ ~

I will tell about the wedding later and how I laughed out loud when the bishop tied my mother and father's hands together with his scarlet sash. Not because of the ceremony but because my philandering brothers and cousin Bunky and my husband, Freddy, *were crying*. Matrimony, monogamy, all the difficult things they sentimentally believed in, but were not very good at practicing. It was a great moment, etched in my memory forever. I have forgotten what I was wearing, that's how important the ceremonious moment became, the ancient ritual, Mother in her blue silk suit, Daddy looking thin and determined, not guilty, but repentant, all the men crying, me laughing so hard I could not stifle the sound, my sons lined up behind my father, his grandchildren, his gene bearers. Up in Jackson my six nieces were probably feeling a chill in their bones, a wind from the south, knowing their indomitable grandfather was on his way home to set things right in their lives and shape them up and for sure get rid of my niece Kathleen's black friends or friend. Odysseus come to kill the lovers.

I think I was wearing a blue print silk dress with a ruffle cut very low and the top of my breasts showing. I had on three-inch heels and was towering over my five-foot-eight-inch wealthy Jewish husband whom I really loved and admired. He adored my family, he adored all my brothers and male cousins and my sons. He was a gem of a husband. I wish I could have kept him and still become a writer but the choice had to be made. I wish I had let him give me some money when I left him to go live in Fayetteville, Arkansas, but I didn't let him and I suppose I'm proud that I didn't take money I had not earned.

My Momma and Daddy Get Married in the Cathedral, Or, Forgive Us Our Trespasses As We Forgive Those Who Trespass Against Us

THE BISHOP OF LOUISIANA TIED THEIR HANDS TOGETHER WITH his golden sash. Momma had been volunteering to help with the bishop's robes at the cathedral during the year she lived in New Orleans. After Daddy got a divorce in Mexico and married Lucy because Momma wouldn't live with him in Wyoming.

Momma loved the beautiful Baptiste and handmade lace gowns that went under the bishop's velvet robes. She saw to it that they were washed by hand and carefully ironed. Also, she attended early communion twice a week and met with the bishop on Saturday afternoons.

My momma was a beautiful lady with the loveliest legs in the American South. More importantly, she was an angel, considered so by everyone who crossed her path. Her nickname was Bodie, which means sweet in classical Greek. My mother's family was from England and studied Greek and Latin from the time they were children.

Bishop Northrup of Christ Church Cathedral in New Orleans was not the first bishop to become Momma's friend. She attended All Saints Episcopal School in Vicksburg where she and her sister lived with the fabled Bishop Green. There were no high schools near the plantation where they grew up. During my childhood the bishop of Mississippi borrowed our summer house on the Alabama coast and performed marriages in our living room when girls in the family had to marry in a hurry. This happened four or five times during my life in Momma and Daddy's house. An ordinary week would be going by, then, suddenly, there would be a wedding. My brother and my friend Mary, my cousin Augusta and my cousin Quart, daughters of my mother's friends. Finally, my outrageously beautiful niece and the governor's youngest son. Most of these weddings took place in Decatur, Alabama, where Daddy made his millions, but later there were weddings in Jackson, Mississippi, after he bought the Caterpillar Tractor dealership there.

The progeny of these couples are a group of young men and women who are exceptionally beautiful and talented and smart. Centuries of literature tell us that children conceived from such passions are always special. Leonardo da Vinci is a case in point.

In the world in which I live now, the twenty-first century, A.D., these shining, fresh, fertilized eggs are mostly aborted, some even cut from their mother's wombs at four or five months. These modern young men and women have better things to do than give birth and care for their young. They plan to write boring books about their boring lives and addictions or paint abstract paintings with dark, sophomoric jokes for titles or train for triathlons or just move back into their parents' houses and smoke dope and occasionally get a job waiting tables or serving coffee in coffee shops.

They are a pleasant, charming group, almost a new cult. They collect Medicaid and college tuition and food stamps from the government and elect whatever politicians will give it to them.

But I am getting away from the story. My angelic mother was remarrying my father in Christ Church Cathedral at eleven in the morning on a cool, glorious April day. In attendance were my two brothers and their current wives, my darling Jewish husband and myself, my cousin Bunky and his young second wife, my Aunt Margaret and my Uncle George, my Aunt Roberta and Uncle Charlie, my maid, Traceleen, my mother's maid, Sophia, four or five of my parents' sixteen grandchildren, including my three sons, and a few of Momma's friends from New Orleans.

When Bishop Northrup took off his sash and tied my Momma's and Daddy's hands together I got so tickled I almost had to leave the church. Most of the men were crying. My husband, Freddy, and my youngest brother and my cousin Bunky were weeping. If my father could be forgiven for getting a Mexican divorce and going off to Wyoming to live with my oldest brother's mother-in-law for ten months, any man could be forgiven for anything and the men in that congregation needed to know such forgiveness was still in the world since they had all had it and at any moment might need it again.

Back to the second wedding of my Momma and Daddy. At Mother's request, Bishop Northrup was conducting the ceremony out of the old Book of Common Prayer, created in the year of our Lord one thousand, seven hundred and eighty-nine by the best writers ever to use the English language, not the watered-down version the church is using now. I met one of the thin, pasty-looking New Englanders who rewrote the Book of Common Prayer in the nineteen eighties to fulfill some outlandish desire to make it more accessible to the social-climbing Baptists who were at that time joining the Episcopal Church in droves. Many of them have become ministers which is why I never go to church anymore.

Momma was wearing pale blue silk, a soft dress just to her knees and pale blue high-heeled slippers that made her seventy-year-old legs even more beautiful than they had been when she was a girl. I inherited those legs and they have opened many doors for me.

Daddy was looking serious in a dark suit and he didn't laugh when the bishop tied their hands together. "This time forever," the bishop said, loudly enough for the congregation to hear.

Daddy really needed Momma to make up with him. My second oldest niece was running around with a wild crowd in Jackson and had been dating black men. Daddy thought if he and Momma moved back into the big house on the farm in Jackson they could corral all the grandchildren and save them from the craziness of the 1970s. He had moved to Wyoming to get all of us away from that craziness but no one would come out there and live with him. We all liked to go there to hunt and ski but we wouldn't move there and run small businesses as he had planned. He offered to buy us small banks and dry cleaning establishments and filling stations but no one took the bait. We could get him to give us anything we wanted where we were. Why should we move to Wyoming and freeze to death?

My two oldest sons stayed the longest in Wyoming. When we caught them using and selling dope in New Orleans we sent them there, singly and together, but it didn't work. When they went to live on Daddy's ranch together they started growing marijuana in an abandoned trailer house behind one of the barns. By the time my younger brother, Bob, went out to visit and found the plants my sons had a thriving business going at Buffalo High School.

Bob said, "When I opened the door there was a forest. They were heating the place with space heaters and had a humidifier going at both ends. I can't believe Daddy or one of the ranch hands didn't notice the smoke. I guess the boys were buying off the ranch hands with product."

"Dearly Beloved, we are gathered together here in the sight of God, and in the face of this company, to join together this Man and this Woman in Holy Matrimony; which is an honorable estate, instituted of God, signifying unto us the mystical union that is betwixt Christ and his Church: which holy estate Christ adorned and beautified with his presence and first miracle that he wrought in Cana of Galilee, and is commended of St. Paul. . . ," the bishop read. A couple of the men were crying already, before he even tied my parents' hands together.

It was a perfect morning, cool and fragrant with lilies on the altar. My Jewish in-laws had sent three dozen lilies to the cathedral. The sunlight shone down from the great stained glass windows upon my parents where they stood before the bishop holding hands. I have never understood how my mother could go through such a fine ceremony and still not allow my father to have a golden anniversary party when the time came. "No," she said, one of the singular mean moments of her life. "He gave up that privilege when he married that woman." The woman was the other grandmother of her first five granddaughters. Another mean thing Momma did was blame one of them for her grandmother's transgression.

"Wilt thou have this Woman to thy wedded wife, to live together after God's ordinance in the holy estate of Matrimony? Wilt thou love her, comfort her, honour and keep her in sickness and in health; and, FORSAKING ALL OTHERS, KEEP THEE ONLY UNTO HER, SO LONG AS YOU BOTH SHALL LIVE."

"I will," my father answered. I guess he was crying too.

We should have had doves released from the ceiling, I was thinking, or at least we should have all the little children here, especially the two babies.

"FORASMUCH AS AURORA AND DOOLEY HAVE CONSENTED TOGETHER IN HOLY WEDLOCK, AND HAVE WITNESSED THE SAME BEFORE GOD AND THIS COMPANY, AND THERETO HAVE GIVEN AND PLEDGED THEIR TROTH, EACH TO THE OTHER, AND HAVE DECLARED THE SAME BY GIVING AND RECEIVING A RING, AND BY JOINING HANDS; I PRONOUNCE THAT THEY ARE MAN AND WIFE, IN THE NAME OF THE FATHER AND OF THE SON AND OF THE HOLY GHOST. AMEN.

"God the Father, God the Son, God the Holy Ghost, bless, preserve, and keep you; the Lord mercifully with his favour look upon you, and fill you with all spiritual benediction and grace. . . ."

My mother and father came down gracefully from the altar and embraced all of us, Bunky and my older brother still crying shamelessly and my aunts hugging my mother with worried faces. They had had their precious Bodie with them for two years, talked her into having a thirty-thousand-dollar face lift, flown to New York City together on private planes, fixed her up with a federal judge she had known at Ole Miss and a retired surgeon she had danced with in the delta when she was young. She had a beautiful apartment, a car service, her daughter, me, around the corner with my wealthy Jewish husband, my youngest son practically living in the basement of her duplex, where, unknown to us, he was running a bar supplied by my husband's wine cellar, but at least he wasn't selling marijuana and at least he wasn't caught until a week after the wedding when Momma packed up her apartment and moved back to the farm in Rankin County to try to save the grandchildren from the madness that was overtaking the world she knew, the world she so fantastically, perfectly represented.

The reception was at my and Freddy's tall stucco house on Story Street. The bishop stayed for several hours and drank several bottles of Piesporter Goldtropfen Freddy's Uncle Irby had supplied for the party. He and Freddy's brothers had not come to the wedding but had been waiting for us at our house getting things ready for the party.

"Life goes by like a dream," Eudora Welty taught me and certainly that day and afternoon and evening have a dreamlike quality in my memory. Not fuzzy. Quite the opposite. I have vivid, lifelike memories of the ceremony and the men crying and my breaking into hysterical laughter and the billowing silk of Mother's dress and the seriousness of my father's face and the beauty and strength and good humor of my family, all still in perfect health and rich in money and power and fun and ideas and the breath coming in and out of our bodies and Uncle Irby's French wines and champagne and the waiters and the food and walking out onto the front porch with my cousin Bunky and savoring all of it and the afternoon going by and everyone's joy at the happy ending. Momma and Daddy back where they were supposed to be in our lives and the Black Witch, Lucy, alone in Nashville with the daughter my older brother had to marry when he was eighteen years old because she was too stupid not to get pregnant and her stupid genes mixed with ours now forever.

The whole time Daddy lived with Lucy I wanted to kill her. I dreamed of it all the time.

Blowjobs, my brothers blamed for the problem. He'd never had one before.

He'd never cheated on her before, we all believed.

~ ~ ~

Now we were all in my and Freddy's house on Story Street with the fabulous French wines and Mother glowing with happiness and only my aunts worrying about anything.

I do not remember much about the evening. My mother and my father and my brothers left at dark and drove home to Jackson, leaving my aunts and me to begin to shut down her apartment.

My darling, funny, brilliant, Exeter- and Harvard-educated, beautiful of face and figure and mind, Jewish husband and I went to bed and played around and made love and he got out his camera and took photographs of me naked in our bed, something he had never asked to do and I still believe it was because he was studying the photographs of Edward Steichen and wanted to do some nudes. When I divorced him a few years later so I could go off and write books to make up for my children embarrassing me to death by selling drugs I went through all his negatives and took the ones of me with no clothes on. Not because I didn't want him to have them but because I thought I was too fat to be in a nude photograph and was afraid they would get into the wrong hands and end up on the cover of *People Magazine*. I had already had enough success to know there was a chance I might get famous and I sure didn't want nude photographs with bunches of fake Chinese violets covering my red pubic hair becoming part of my fame.

I never tore them up, however. I am looking at two of them now, forty-seven years later and to tell the truth I don't look very fat, maybe seven pounds of unnecessary flesh but not ten, maybe not even seven since I was running nine miles a day at the time they were taken and most of it is muscle.

Freddy is dead now, of a terrible and fast-acting leukemia and Bunky died the other day and I had to go to his funeral in the same cathedral where my Momma and Daddy got married for the second time. Uncle George and Aunt Margaret are dead and Aunt Roberta and Uncle Charlie and Mr. and Mrs. Kullman and Freddy's Uncle Irby. The names of the lost go on and on and on.

It was during Bunky's funeral, surrounded by his four sons, by my cousin Abigail and his second wife, which love story I told in "The Famous Poll at Jody's Bar," and their daughter, Sissy, and many of his grandchildren and all three of my sons and their children and grandchildren and living cousins, men who adored me and still adore me but I couldn't concentrate on the living and count my blessings. I just kept calling on the dead to come back and live with us again and not die and not go to heaven and leave us only our myriad, amazing, wonderful, fabulous, heavenly memories of all we had and did and were and said and drank and ate and walked and ran and sailed and skied and drove and cars we wrecked and walked away from and airplanes we chartered and owned and flew and sailboats we sailed in storms, and diamonds and gold bracelets and paintings we bought and gave away and artists we supported and work we did and goddamn it to heaven, blessings, blessings, blessings.

I decided to try to write some of it down before the oxygen stops pouring into my lungs and nourishing my blood and feeding the unbelievable storehouse of my seventy-eight-year-old brain. Here it is. Everything I can remember as fast as I can write it down.

Further In and Deeper Out (Wyoming)

WE WERE A PARTY OF THIRTEEN IN THREE VEHICLES. MY MOTHER, Aurora Alford Gilchrist, my father, William Garth Gilchrist, Jr. (Big Dooley), my brother Bob Gilchrist, my brother William Garth Gilchrist III (Little Dooley), and four of his daughters, Ellen, Lucy, Penny, and Cindy, his second wife, Sandra (mother of Penny and Cindy), myself, Ellen Gilchrist, and my three sons, Pierre, Garth, and Marshall Walker.

Thirteen was not a problem for us. My father was born on January 13, 1908. He had always told us thirteen was our lucky number.

We were going north and west from Casper, Wyoming, to Jackson Hole, Wyoming, and then further west to the Grand Targhee Ski Resort in Driggs, Idaho.

It was a five-and-a-half-hour drive to Jackson Hole. How we got there. Highway 25 to Riverton, then to DuBois, then Moran, then south for forty miles to Jackson Hole. We stopped in Moran late in the afternoon to ski the dangerous steep runs the resort was famous for. Garth and Marshall loved the black runs and skied them until it was dark. When I was coming down a blue run I saw a huge thermometer that said minus 20 degrees Fahrenheit.

We skied Jackson Hole for four days. Marshall and Garth were out on the black runs all day. Strange to remember that I never worried about them. Pierre and the girls were taking turns skiing and buying things in the ski lodges. We would meet at night to eat real meals but the rest of the time they were feeding themselves in the warming huts at the top of the runs.

I was getting up at dawn to be the first person on the slopes. I loved being the first person to break new snow.

Four days later we went to Driggs, Idaho, to the Grand Targhee Ski Resort. To this day I think it is the best skiing in the world, long fields of snow that you can take forever to come down. I went back one time at Easter with Pierre and Little Ellen and had a wonderful time skiing with Scandinavian ski instructors while Ellen and Pierre went from warming lodge to warming lodge eating and buying things. On Easter Sunday the instructors skied in bathing suits.

Coming back from Targhee in the late afternoon of the Christmas trip, I was in the Mercedes with Dooley driving, Sandra in the front passenger seat, and Garth and me in the back. Dooley saw a moose on a mountain. We were on a long, narrow overpass that was covered with snow and it was getting dark. The overpass had almost no shoulders and steep drops on both sides.

Dooley turned around to tell Garth to look at the moose and the Mercedes slid off the road and went down about twenty feet, sliding in the heavy snow. I definitely thought we were dying and the car filled with white light and I had my first near-death experience.

Dooley remembers this very differently. He says the car's front wheel hit a slick spot and only slid about five feet down the hill in the snow.

One way or the other my father was behind us in the pickup truck and stopped and he and my brother and some state troopers got us out of the Mercedes and into the back of the pickup truck camper with some of the children. I was freezing all the way home and had pneumonia when I got back to New Orleans four days later. I have always blamed the pneumonia on riding home in the camper.

We arrived at the house in Casper in a snowstorm and went inside and went to sleep.

The next morning was Christmas Eve. We worked all day getting ready for Christmas Day.

On Christmas Day we woke at dawn and the children opened their presents and ate chocolate candy ornaments off the tree and everything was very merry until my brother and my father caught Marshall and Garth smoking marijuana in the downstairs bathroom.

After that there was a lot of yelling and screaming and in the end I took my two oldest sons and my husband and flew home that night to New Orleans. Pierre stayed to ski Casper Mountain with his cousins.

This was at the very beginning of the dope problems with my sons. They were thirteen and fourteen. I wish now I had let my father and my brother yell at them and threaten them and lock them up. It was stupid of me to protect them. My husband, Freddy, and I were not capable of disciplining them. If I had let Daddy and my brothers work on them at that point in their lives I might have saved us all many lost years of bad grades, being kicked out of colleges, psychiatry, and all the other things that had to happen before they belatedly grew up and became the fine men they are now.

This was happening all around me in New Orleans with children of all classes and colors. The seventies had come and the hippies were living in Audubon Park and the Pied Piper came and stole the children. We are lucky. We got ours back. Some of them died. Many never got straight. All of them were damaged, even the luckiest of them. The real damage was to the polite, disciplined, hard-fought-for culture of the United States.

I see the aftermath in my students in 2010. They drink, take drugs, write about drinking and taking drugs, and seem to have no hope of living useful, successful lives.

And on and on and on. So it was with Athens, with Rome, with the British Empire, now it is the United States's turn. Maybe we'll make it. Maybe we won't. I hope to God we do. My brother Dooley has twenty grandchildren, Bob has two, I have fifteen. I wish we could leave them the strong, disciplined world we knew. Some of them will know it, some of the older ones already have.

I am fighting for them with all the strength and hope and words on paper I can find. I hate drugs and alcohol and all the things that destroy young minds. I hate political correctness with its myriad lies and distortions. Tell the truth, for God's sake, tell the truth.

"This above all to thine own self be true and thou canst not then be false to any man." William Shakespeare.

Writing Maketh an Exact Man

———— ⌘ ————

IT IS IMPORTANT TO WRITE DOWN IMPORTANT MEMORIES, TO store them on paper as well as in our mortal brains. The idea of people in the future finding pieces of paper we left behind has always fascinated me. Who will someday dig up my and Connie Beth Ingram's and Cynthia Hancock's time capsule in Harrisburg, Illinois? Who will unearth the one Donna Dustin and Donna Brummette and I left in Seymour, Indiana, during a cold February day in the middle of the Second World War? I was hoping it wouldn't be Japanese soldiers but you had to be prepared for any eventuality. I was in the second grade and fiercely self-protective. I was ready to be nice to the conquerors, learn their language, teach them to plant corn and carrots, show them where there were orchards, how to run the projector at Connie Beth's father's outdoor picture show. I worked at the concession stand when I spent the night with Connie and knew all about how to show the movies.

There would be no need to kill a useful little girl like me. I could saddle horses, change tires on trucks, make mayonnaise, learn languages. I was studying Latin with my mother and she said if I learned it I could learn any Romance language easily. I knew Japanese wasn't a Romance language but chose to ignore that information as I lay in bed at night planning what to do if we lost the war.

~ ~ ~

My father was not afraid we would lose the war. It worried him that the government spent too much money doing things but since he was one of the ones who built the army and air force bases and poured the concrete runways where we taught young men to fly airplanes, he did his job eighteen hours a day no matter how many wasteful frills the government made him add to the bases, such as canteens for the officers and soldiers. His brother was a pilot and his cousins were soldiers. They were Scots like him. They didn't need canteens. They needed to get the job done and get on to the next job. Get up, eat breakfast, go to work building a military for the United States of America. Go home, have one drink, eat dinner, call your children in one by one and ask questions and give advice, say your prayers, especially for the safety of all our soldiers and your brother and your cousins, go to sleep, get up in the middle of the night and drink water and make lists for the next day, go back to sleep, get up at five o'clock and go to work.

Forty-five years later my father had not changed one iota. He lived on war time with war rations. Same khaki pants, same belt, same ironed white shirts, same white tee-shirts, same pencils and pens and folded envelope in his left-hand shirt pocket, same short beige jacket in case it got cold, same jewelry, an Auburn class ring.

He had made several million dollars but had never spent a cent of it on himself except to buy a ranch in Buffalo, Wyoming, and a lot of ski equipment at yard sales in Buffalo. He bought horses but mostly he bartered for them.

My mother didn't let him live on the ranch long. By the time he was eighty he was back in her house in Jackson, Mississippi spending his time and energy taking care of his fifteen grandchildren and six great-grandchildren and buying houses and cars for people who needed them. He bought real estate and a huge place for all of us to be buried. He turned all his investments into gold coins and couldn't believe the rest of us wouldn't do so too.

He liked to get people alone with him on car trips and talk to them about the federal reserve and the need to buy and hold gold coins in bank vaults and home safes. He liked to get my husband's law partners to build secret vaults in fireplaces in which to store gold coins. Many of them did it. They thank me for that every time I run into them.

I lived four hundred and fifty miles away from my parents in a mountainous town in northwestern Arkansas that was hard to drive or fly to. I didn't want Daddy coming to see me or giving me advice about God and money management.

I drove the eight hours down to Jackson every month. There were always birthdays or celebrations or weddings or reasons to go see about my own children and grandchildren.

I couldn't work around them. There was too much energy and testosterone and estrogen and teenage crises and new babies and wives and new husbands going on in my family to get anything imaginative done. The reality was way more exciting than anything I could think up or write down.

Sometimes Daddy needed me to do something for him. The phone call would come at seven in the morning. "Sister," he would say. "I need you to do something for me."

I would always go and do it. No matter how much it messed up a good writing spell or any work I had to do, I got in the car and drove down to Jackson to do whatever my daddy needed.

One of my great memories of doing things for Daddy was a January day in 1996. He was eighty-six years old. He had had a pacemaker for several years, had been having trouble with his arm and leg, his unbelievably strong arm and leg, and he wanted to go to Cleveland, Mississippi, to have lunch with his (all male) first cousins at the Cleveland Country Club. I had just won several big awards for writing and they wanted to talk to me, which was why I had to be the driver and not one of my brothers.

His cousin Charles Clark, who was chief justice of the Fifth Circuit Court of Appeals, would be there. His beloved cousin Lavalle House, who had gone to Annapolis and then to the Korean War where he contracted polio and came home a decorated hero with a rank of lieutenant commander. His mother met him at the boat in New Orleans, bought them a house and they lived in New Orleans while he learned to be a librarian at Tulane University. Then he and his mother went home to Cleveland, Mississippi where he was the base librarian at an army base near Cleveland. He hired an architect and rebuilt his family's white board mansion into a wheelchair-accessible place to live. When it was done he could leave his third-floor bedroom, go down an outside elevator to a chute that took him to his automobile where his wheelchair was lifted automatically into the car and fitted behind the steering apparatus and the gas pedal controls. Then he drove himself to work.

My father and the other cousins worshipped Lavalle. He was a beautiful and charismatic man and I fell in love with him every time I was in his presence. He had an ability to make you know how vitally interested he was in you that I have never seen again except in Bill Clinton, whom I know and also love.

There were many other powerful exciting men at the meeting of the cousins. Their wives were there also but I didn't notice them.

These were the sons of my grandmother, Louise Clark Gilchrist, and of her sisters, all descendants of General Charles Clark who was the wartime governor of the state of Mississippi during the Civil War.

How did these women raise all those sons to be such useful and powerful members of their society? One was the speaker of the House of Representatives of the state of Mississippi, one a physician who became president of the state, county, and local medical societies, my father, a Caterpillar Tractor dealer and philanthropist, a colonel in the United States Air Force who flew bombing missions over Germany and then flew with the Flying Tigers in Asia under General Claire Chennault. Two or three generations of lawyers in Cleveland and surrounding towns, whose daughters would also become lawyers.

I know it began with discipline, self-discipline and high expectations and a work ethic that always finds fertile soil in men and women with Scots genes.

Next was a learned devotion to good deeds and courage and a sense of responsibility to the society as a whole. These were deeply held Presbyterian beliefs. Presbyterians believe they are a chosen people, chosen by God to lead others to charity and goodness and hard work. You don't have a choice if you are a Presbyterian. You have to work hard all your life to make the world a better place. You have to live up to expectations. My father's father used to say he would rather have a son of his be dead than be a drunkard. I share that feeling and wish more people admitted that's the way they feel.

Good deeds are what my father did. He did them every day and to anyone he met. He picked up hitchhikers until the day my brothers took away his car. He burned the skin off his hands pulling a truck driver from a burning truck he saw crash on the highway. His hands healed. It wouldn't have mattered if they hadn't healed. He did what his upbringing told him to do.

I think about those women a lot, Grannie Clark Gilchrist and her Clark sisters who became Houses and Allens. There were also Clark cousins as the girls had had a brother.

I think more than any other thing these women taught by example. They were educated women and they continued to educate themselves. They read books and magazines and newspapers. They kept up with the world even when they didn't approve of where it was going.

Their own lives were examples of thrift, good humor, kind words and deeds, good works, and church attendance. They kept up with each other's families and were always ready to lend a hand in emergencies.

What a lucky girl I was to have these women for my role models. It took awhile for the lessons of their lives to make sense to me. I had to have it taught to me the hard way but I did learn it. I am trying to make my old age an example for any young people who pass my way. Pass it on, my mother's Episcopalian Church says, when they pass the peace.

Pass it on. Pray for peace. Good will toward men.

ADDENDA

I know a secret about how parents teach children their culture and belief systems and good manners and morals and ways of being. In the first place the DNA is there with the blueprint of what your people learned and knew and believed. In the second place, if they are good parents, the examples they set, day after day, month after month, year after year, are teaching and imprinting unforgettable knowledge. My parents taught me how to be old and how to be courageous in the face of the problems aging brings. If you are really lucky the things your parents teach are the way they are. They aren't telling you one thing and doing another.

I always *talked back* to both my parents, especially my mother, and told them the advice they were giving me was wrong or imprecise or *out of date* but they just kept on telling me the same things over and over again, and, of course, it turned out everything they told me was right and as the years go by I do what they told me to do. This is advice to parents I am giving right now. Go on and keep saying it and they won't forget it and when they need it it will be there, reinforcing the blueprint in the genes.

My parents and grandparents and the great-grandparent and great-great-grandparent that I knew well were all teaching the same Christian ideas, which other cultures share, about being kind and being forgiving and working for other people and helping other people and, from my father, tithing, an idea he loved because he made a lot of money and he loved to give it away to people who needed it.

Both he and my mother devoted their lives to their progeny and to anyone who worked for or with them. Money and property were to be shared with other people. My father loved a place called Boys Town and kept a photograph of a young man with a child on his shoulders on his desk. It never occurred to either of my parents to not help people in need, whether it was with advice and help or with money.

What they didn't tell me is that generosity makes you happy. There is nothing in the world more fulfilling than to right wrongs or fill needs.

Albert Einstein took that idea further. He said nothing in life makes people happier than to be involved with other people in a project that makes life better for everyone.

Another gift my parents gave me is a sense of humor. I really do see the whole show as fabulously amusing. I was out for a walk one afternoon recently and was walking behind a pair of lovely young women. I wasn't eavesdropping. I was just looking for a way to pass them on the walking path without being rude.

"I'll tell you one thing," the tall blonde said to her friend. "This day has been a complete waste of makeup."

Human beings are just too good to be true, most of the time. As for the bad ones, I don't know. Personally I stay away from them and am grateful to the men and women who protect us from them.

No end to that discussion.

As for your children. Love them until the day you die or they die. If they need anything give it to them before they can ask. Then they will do the same for their children and the DNA will keep on keeping you alive forever. I believe that, so I am not afraid of death. So what, I say to death. I always did love to sleep. Just bury me near my mother and my daddy near the huge gravestone my father had made with the names of his male ancestors going all the way back to Scotland.

If I have time before I die I'm going to get a piece of Carrera marble and have it engraved with my female ancestors going back to Scotland and England and Ireland and Wales and put it near Daddy's wonderful stone. Not for any reason, just for a joke.

A Store of Treasures

WHEN I WAS EIGHT YEARS OLD I BURIED A TIME CAPSULE IN MY backyard. I can remember every minute of that day. I can remember I was wearing a plaid dress. I can remember going up the stairs to my room and searching for things to include. I can remember carrying the capsule out to the yard and digging the hole and putting it in and covering it up and patting down the earth but I cannot remember what was in it, except perhaps my Girl Scout badge and a copy of the photograph I had mailed to Margaret O'Brien to thank her for the one she mailed to me after I wrote her a fan letter for her role in *Journey for Margaret.*

What did I put in that time capsule? God only knows. I hated to part with my prized possessions but I wanted it to contain enough so the future would think well of me and know I was educated. Of course, I must have written something. I thought of myself as a writer and wrote things all the time. I would not have minded parting with something I wrote, as I knew I could write it again anytime I liked. Even though we were in a war and everything was rationed I always had plenty of paper and pencils.

I would give anything to have that time capsule. It's somewhere in a backyard in Seymour, Indiana, on a rise of land, behind the remains of a victory garden and near the alley where I once found a card shuffler. I doubt if much remains of it since it was buried in a cardboard matchbox. There is a chance, however, that I had some sort of tin box covering the matchbox because I remember my brother Dooley telling me that it wasn't going to last. During those years I was obsessed with impermanence and the imminence of death and loss. We were in the middle of a world war, my uncles were flying bombing missions over Germany, everything was rationed, and we had moved ten times in my eight years of life. My father was in charge of building airports to train the pilots to fly the airplanes men and women were building in places like Seattle, Washington, and Lansing, Michigan.

The reason I was making the time capsule was because of the war, plus some other sad things that had happened in my family. They tried to keep those things from me but children are smart. They are always listening, especially if anything is being said in low voices, or being whispered. Especially if it makes their mother cry. Her father had died in the delta the year before. A few months later my paternal grandfather died in Alabama. My parents had looks on their faces that said it might not be safe in the world, no matter how many hours we spent on our knees at the Episcopal Church, praying for help from the skies.

It was coming from the skies all right. From the B-54 bombers my uncle was flying over the factories in Alsace-Lorraine, from the concrete runways my father was building as fast as they could be built, from the paper drives I had and the sugar my mother saved. I was a war girl. I helped with the war. If they had given me a gun I would have loved to shoot it at our enemies. When I see twelve-year-old boys learning war at camps in Palestine I know who they are. I was fierce like that and longing to participate.

So I buried a time capsule, just in case I should die and have no memorial. I wanted a memorial. I wanted the future to know I had existed.

I don't know where I got the idea for a time capsule. Maybe from the newspapers my father and I read assiduously every morning. Maybe from a magazine although I don't remember there being many magazines during the war. Perhaps I heard about time capsules on one of the radio programs Dooley and I listened to at night. Anyway, I thought up making one, dressed in my favorite red and green plaid dress, ate breakfast and went to work. By noon I was out in the yard digging the hole. I loved to dig in the earth and had spent my early childhood trying to make it down to China.

My father was an engineer and our tool shed was always full of shovels and posthole diggers. I remember the earth was very hard that day and I had to dig for a long time to scrape out a place deep enough for my box. I put it in, covered it up, patted down the earth and replaced a scrap of grass to keep it secret. Dooley was sitting on the back steps laughing at me but I didn't care. He could take his chances with the future. I was making sure I'd be remembered.

I wonder what I would include if I were burying a time capsule today. A few of my books, photographs of my progeny, a pair of my old eyeglasses, what else? I'm sure it would contain the four teeth I had removed yesterday morning. I had been dreading and preparing myself for those extractions for days. Dozens of times I woke up in the middle of the night having magnified the occasion into great pain and suffering, dry sockets that would never heal, a future as a tooth-less hag, my cheeks sunken in, only will left to get me through a horrible old age with no smile, no teeth, or worse, some sort of prosthetic device in my mouth that would alter my speech. I would never be able to speak in public again. I would lisp. I would spit. Food would fall from my mouth. I would attempt to put soup in my mouth and the soup would dribble out and fall on my breast. Still, I am nothing if not a survivor. Go back to sleep, I would tell myself. I refuse to have bad dreams.

While I waited for the horrible day I exercised two hours a day. I wanted my body to be ready for the surgery, tuned up. I wanted my immune system to be at fever pitch. It was not as if a range of possibilities was open to me. I had four infected teeth that had had everything done to them that dental science could think of to do.

Every root had either been incised or had a root canal. There was nothing left to do but take the teeth out or die of infection. So the teeth were coming out. I was going to put as good a face on this as possible. I became adjusted to the idea of being a toothless hag. I began to like the idea. Think what a good example I will set for other people, I decided, when I refuse to be made unhappy by being a toothless hag. When I flaunt being a toothless hag. When I refuse to wear the miserably uncomfortable prosthetic device and go around toothless as in an old Greek play.

It has now been forty-eight hours since my teeth were removed. The whole procedure took thirty minutes. I only had to have one shot of Novocain. I was in absolutely no pain whatsoever. The device that had been made for me to wear in place of my teeth fit perfectly into my mouth. I like it! I can talk! I can eat! It fits! It stays there! It's darling! It looks a lot better than those ugly, ugly, ugly teeth that I struggled so hard to preserve. And this is not even the permanent device. This is a temporary partial plate that I was supposed to find unwieldy and uncomfortable. And I never, never, never have to thread dental floss through the crown and bridgework again as long as I live which means I don't have to watch television if I don't want to. I used to have to watch television to amuse myself while I flossed. It was so boring to have to floss those old, terrible, crowned teeth that I would have to turn the television on while I did it. I became addicted to late afternoon news programs. I figured the totally boring activity of flossing my teeth plus the totally boring activity of watching the afternoon news programs would cancel each other out the way two minuses make a plus. Like two negative charges make a positive charge, only it didn't work. All that happened was I got addicted to talking heads. By the time I finished flossing I would be caught up in some inane television program, filling my mind with murder, abused children, mayhem, civil riots. Now all I have to do is take this beautiful little piece of hardware out of my mouth and clean it, as I would a shoe with a brush.

This is a moral lesson. I feel like a new person. I had my piano tuned. I don't know what to do with myself. I think I'll go to Europe. No, I'll just stay here and learn to play Satie's *Gymnopédie*, No. 1, on my piano. I have been sick and now I'm well.

OCTOBER 10, 2002

Living in the Shadow of
a Beautiful Mother

⟵•⟶

IT ISN'T SO MUCH HER BEAUTY AS IT IS HER PERFECTION. IT IS always the classic moment with my mother; the exact right amount of perfume, the perfect nail color, the simple perfect bracelet, the ladylike hemlines. Of course, there was nothing left for me to do but rebel. To this date, at age fifty-six, mind you, nothing pleases me more than to be able to put on an obscenely short micro-mini and wear it out to breakfast on Sunday morning. *What is a woman that old doing in a skirt that short?* I imagine people saying.

I know my mother will hear about it, sooner or later, down in Jackson, Mississippi, where she is still wielding unquestioned editorial power over the hemlines and haircuts of my nine nieces, two sisters-in-law, three ex-sisters-in-law, and countless great-granddaughters and cousins. "I saw a picture of Ellen in *People Magazine* wearing some weird denim vest," one of her bridge partners will surely tell her. "I guess she's never going to cut her hair."

The women in my family bring everything they buy to my mother's house to model for her and await her judgment. She doesn't even buy all those clothes for them anymore. Still, they await her approval like runway models getting the nod from Calvin. They do this with good reason. My mother is a fashion genius, descended from a long line of fabulous seamstresses. The foot-pedal sewing machines hum in her brain. She has an unerring eye for cut and style and color, and, like a good editor, she never tells a lie, even to spare the wearer's feelings. "That color isn't good for you," she will say. Or, "that makes your hips look big." Or, "you can do better than that, my darling.

Take that back to the store." It isn't easy to win her approval. As I said, she stops at the classic moment.

Even though I live four hundred miles away, I am still not free from the compulsion to win her approval. When it comes to a big occasion, a public appearance in a town where I have friends, or, sometimes, just to report on a successful shopping expedition, I find myself calling to talk to her about clothes. I will describe the dress or outfit that I bought and answer questions about shoes, accessories, handbags, scarves, hose, jewelry, *hemlines*. "Don't get it too short," she will say several times, no matter how much I prevaricate on the answer. "Not above the knee. Don't get it too short. It's so common, honey."

As I said, she is descended from a long line of seamstresses and she can *envision* cut and style and line and color. *She can envision hems.* Her great-grandmother, who lived in perfect health until I was four, was a milliner from Wilkes-Barre, Pennsylvania. This woman came down the Monongahela and Ohio and Mississippi rivers after the Civil War and, with her husband and their companions, settled the little town of Mayersville, Mississippi. She brought with her patterns and knowledge of fashion and passed it on to her three daughters, who passed it on to my mother, who has tried to teach it to me.

Of course, the clothes and hats and hairdos and buttons and rickrack and lace are all great fun, greatly beautiful, and undeniably an art form, but it would be a mistake to think they constitute the *thing* that was beautiful about these women or the thing that made them loved. The clothes were "an outward and visible sign of an inward and spiritual grace."

When we see something that is truly beautiful we know the maker created it out of love and we return that love. We know this because it is the way we operate ourselves. When we are happy and at peace with ourselves we create beauty. It is that impetus or inspiration that the viewer or watcher responds to. When we see a fabulous garden we share in the moments of inspiration and planning and creation. The same is true when we see a beautiful woman all dressed up with her makeup on and her hair done. The closer the inspiration was to pure happiness or joy, the closer the result will be to beauty. "Euclid alone has looked on Beauty bare," Edna Millay wrote. "Fortunate they who though once only and then but far away, have heard her massive sandal set on stone."

The thing that people find beautiful about my mother is her excitement and energy and grace, her awe, her love of flowers and children and small birds, her sense of order, the delicacy of her language, the kindness and thoughtfulness of her ways. "All along it was indwelling," another poet, Denise Levertov, wrote. "A gold ring lost in the house."

My mother doesn't buy expensive clothes. She thinks it is terrible to spend large sums of money on herself when there are all those young women in the family to buy things for. She likes to shop carefully. She likes to pore over catalogs in the evenings, waiting to spot the exactly perfect dress. Then she will order it and *hem it* and look marvelous in it. It will be very simple, with simple classic lines and she will search around her perfectly ordered closet and find the exact right shoes and scarf and earrings to wear with it. She doesn't make mistakes. I have never known her to buy anything she didn't actually wear. But then she wears her best clothes all day long. She puts them on in the morning and wears them out into the garden and to the grocery store and just to sit in the den and talk to little children. "All along it was indwelling. A gold ring lost in the house."

Great beauty always begins with great physical health. My mother got that in the genes from those same long-lived seamstresses and she takes care of her inheritance. At eighty-three she is still in perfect health and still perfectly beautiful. The natural beauty is there, of course, the high cheekbones, the gorgeous legs, the long graceful arms and hands. She was always a dancer and she moves with a dancer's grace. My father first saw her dancing in a Charleston contest. He watched from the back of the auditorium, then went to work to make friends with her brother. Some weeks later he was brought to her house to be introduced. It was sixty-four years later, on a rainy night in Jackson, Mississippi, when my mother finally heard this story. My mother, my father, my son and myself were on our way to a seven o'clock screening of *Crocodile Dundee.* "Dundee," my father said. "That's the name of the town where we lived the first year we were married."

"How did you meet Grandmother?" my son asked.

"I saw her dancing in a Charleston contest," Daddy answered. "I said to a friend, who's that girl?"

"That's Aurora Alford," he said. "Floyd Alford's sister from the delta."

"You never told me that," my mother put in. "You saw me before Floyd brought you home?"

"Of course I did," my father answered. "Why do you think I was there?"

Great beauty has its drawbacks, of course. Even the most beautiful among us fear the ravages of time. The last person I would ever have been able to imagine giving in to that was my mother. Yet even our mothers turn out to be human. (Feet of clay, I had a character say in a book. It's a clay universe, another character answers.)

It is like the memory of a bad dream when I recall the time my mother went to get a facelift. This was twenty years ago when face-lifts were still fairly unusual things to do. Her sisters were elated. They felt they had sent a scout to the cutting edge of the beauty business. But I was in a funk. There was my mother, *my ground of being,* propped up on the pillows in her pressure bandages. Her beautiful sisters were all around her, worshipping at her daring. "She did it," they kept saying. "She really did it. Can you believe she did it?"

"No," I said, getting furious. "Beauty is one thing. Elective surgery is another." I dropped my flowers at her feet and stormed out of the room and I didn't see her again until the bandages were off and she was almost healed. "How could you do that?" I said when I saw her. "How could a woman your age be that crazy?"

Now, years later, I am the age she was then and I wonder if my anger was at the danger I thought she had put herself in or simply that I knew no matter how much I wanted to, I would never have the courage to let someone cut into me that close to my eyes or my brain.

Of course she looked absolutely marvelous after the stitches healed. She looked ten years younger and never seemed to miss the time or money she had spent. I'm still jealous of this facelift business. Even if I wanted to do it, and if I had the courage, I would not be able to. My psychoanalyst won't let me. He's a hard man. No drinking, no smoking, no facelifts, no breast implants, if you want access to that office. He's not as beautiful as my mother, but he's a lot fiercer and even more protective.

Being raised by a woman who worships beauty has other drawbacks besides the obvious one of not being able to measure up to the standard. Every Halloween of my life I have had to be a beautiful princess. I cannot imagine going to a costume party as a witch or a goblin or a joke. My mother always started weeks ahead making my Halloween costumes. I would be a beautiful antebellum princess or a beautiful princess out of King Arthur's court, with a conical hat and tulle floating down and a blue silk dress with a train. Or I would be a beautiful Oriental princess or a flower girl or a junior bridesmaid or a bride.

Recently I was down on the Mississippi coast with my grandchildren on Halloween. My daughter-in-law, whose ancestors were scientists and artists in New Jersey, had dressed up my granddaughter as a pumpkin. I was shocked. Imagine a little girl not being a beautiful princess? A whole new world of possibilities opened before my eyes and I sat around all evening pondering the limiting aspects of perfectionism and beauty.

I remember a role I had in a fifth-grade play. The play was called *Fire Hazards* and was produced under the auspices of the fire department. I was chosen to play "Spontaneous Combustion." All was going well until they told me I had to wear rags and sit in a garbage can on the stage. I quit the production. It was impossible for me to sit on a stage in such a guise.

I remembered the long mornings I would spend with my little friends Jean Finney and Donna Brummette playing dress-up with my mother's old clothes. "Who is the most beautiful girl in the world?" I would demand. "You are, Ellen," Donna and Jean would reply. Sometimes Donna would refuse to say it. Then I would sit on her until she did.

I even had to have beautiful dolls. Sometimes the dolls were beautifully dressed. If they weren't, my mother would get out her sewing machine and begin to make clothes for them. Unfortunately, I liked naked dolls. The minute a doll arrived I would take off her clothes and put her to bed. "Stay there until I get back," I would say. "I'll be back in a little while." I had a row of doll beds on the back porch piled up with naked dolls. My mother loves to tell the story of the day the Episcopal minister came to call and I took him out on the porch and introduced him to all my naked children. I never have been able to see the humor in that story, although I suppose the point is that the minister, like any good Anglican of that time, wanted the savages to be fully clad.

Another story my mother loves to tell is about the Christmas of 1943, right in the middle of the Second World War, when everything was rationed and people made their Christmas presents. My mother and two of her younger friends had spent a month making a chest of doll clothes to accompany a beautiful black-haired doll an older friend was giving me. There were evening dresses and silk nightgowns and even a coat with a real fur collar and cuffs. Christmas came and there was my doll with her unbelievable wardrobe. They had also found somewhere a toy washing machine and painted and fixed it up for me. It had a real hose and could be filled with real water.

At two o'clock that afternoon my mother found me out on the back porch in the freezing cold weather happily stuffing the last article of doll's clothes into the washing machine. The beautiful doll lay on the floor, asleep and naked, and the fabulous handmade wardrobe was now a wad of ivory soap and water. "I wept," she says, when she tells the story. "It was right in the middle of the war."

When I am thinking deeply and philosophically about beauty I try to ponder the question of illusion. My mother's beauty is not illusory but the enhancement of it certainly is. And the true downside of this endless search for and insistence upon beauty is that it has taught me to judge things by appearances. I was thinking of this the other night. It was eleven o'clock and I had turned on the television to see if the world was still at peace before I went to bed for the night. I was switching channels and came upon a strange and interesting program I have seen by accident several times. A program on PBS called *Thinking Aloud*. It is a program of interviews with philosophers and gurus. The host had just introduced the night's guest, an unattractive man with bad teeth and an awkward ungainly body. Ichabod Crane, I remember thinking. What a strange-looking man. Then the man began to speak. He had just come from spending years in a Zen monastery and had returned to the world to try to teach people to love themselves and one another. He spoke movingly of the possibilities for understanding, the hope that the human race would evolve into more profound and loving creatures. I was spellbound. For the next thirty minutes I barely moved as I listened to this lovely man talk about human dreams. I completely forgot his teeth or the structure of his face or his ungainly posture. He had captured my imagination at a level that was beyond appearances. He had given me the idea that mankind could become more gentle, that happiness and understanding were possible goals for an individual or the race.

The best beauty tip I ever received was from a gorgeous aging model in Dallas. How do you do it? I had asked her. How do you stay so gorgeous, year after year? It's all illusion, she said. Never forget that. Create an illusion and the rest will follow.

An outward and visible sign of an inward and spiritual grace? Of course. The illusion carries *the light of the inspiration* into the physical world. If your boyfriend is coming over at six o'clock and you think you aren't pretty enough to make him love you, here is what you should do. Light candles, straighten up the house, put on music, put flowers on the table, roll up your hair and put on makeup and the prettiest, most colorful clothes that you have. *Overdo it.* Do every charming thing you can imagine. Not for the boyfriend and not even for yourself, really, but *for the sake of beauty itself*, the charming and illusory muse.

I would like to end this story with an interview I conducted with the daughter of the most beautiful woman in the town where I live. This woman is so lovely I put her photograph on the cover of one of my books. "How does it feel to live with a woman as beautiful as your mother?" I asked her thirteen-year-old daughter, Annabelle.

"Well, she's always complaining that she's fat."

"Right," I said. "Go on."

"She's always saying she's getting wrinkled and old, but I don't see any wrinkles. Of course she doesn't dance anymore and I guess that makes her feel old."

"Go on. What else?"

"Strange people come up to me and say, oh, you're Gay's daughter. It's so weird. It's like they don't even know my name."

"Anything else?"

"Well, she's got more clothes than anyone I've ever seen, but she always says she doesn't have anything to wear."

"You don't have to be beautiful for that."

"It's more like she doesn't realize it. Like she doesn't even care."

"Oh, Annabelle," I answered. "Thank you for that. That's the key, isn't it? The thing that makes great beauties truly beautiful. I called up my mother yesterday and told her I was going to write an article about living in the shadow of a beautiful mother and you know what she said? She said, 'Well, I don't know who that could be.' She really meant it. She really doesn't know how much we love to look at her."

This is the woman who let me get a permanent wave when I was five years old. There was a girl in my kindergarten class whose mother owned a beauty parlor and she had a permanent wave. I was so jealous of her curly hair I could hardly sleep at night. I began to campaign, to beg, cry, whine, pout, plead, hide behind the sofa, cajole. My mother, who is a pushover in the child discipline department, caved in quickly and the next Saturday morning I was delivered to the beauty salon and set up underneath the permanent wave machine to get my curls. The beauty parlor was next door to my father's office, in a wooden building with a boardwalk built up over the dirt street. This was 1940 and we were living in Mound City, Illinois, where my father was working for the Corps of Engineers building levees on the Mississippi River.

My mother kissed me goodbye and went off to do errands. The beauty parlor operator gave me a Coke to drink and began to apply huge steel rollers to my hair. Operator had real meaning in those days, as the permanent wave machine was a huge apparatus that had to be constantly monitored so that it wouldn't "frizz" the hair. The operator had rolled the left side of my head when I began to panic. All of a sudden I realized that I couldn't move. I was caught, trapped, held, in the steel embrace. A dozen steel hands had me *by the hair*. I began to scream at the top of my lungs. I screamed louder and louder. "Take it off," I was screaming. "Stop doing this to me. Let me go."

My father was next door in his office and heard my screams and came tearing through the screen doors to save me. "Get that child out of there," he was screaming. "Who would do such a thing to a little girl?" Ten minutes later I was sitting in his lap in his big office chair, my head against his chest, my hand on his arm, and he was giving me sips of water from a little triangular-shaped paper cup. Best of all, he was mad at my mother. "Goddammit, Bodie," he said, when she finally appeared and heard the story. "I can't believe anyone could be that dumb. Spending hard-earned money to torture a little girl." I smiled and turned my face deeper into his soft white shirt. "You are right," my mother might have answered if she had known what I know now. "Distorting her sense of reality, not to mention half of her hair is permed and the other half is not."

Fifty years later the karma caught up with me. It was another Saturday morning and my daughter-in-law called me from the coast. "Guess what?" she said. "Your granddaughter talked me into letting her pierce her ears."

"Oh, no," I answered. "I can't stand it. She's only six years old."

"She wore me down. She begged and begged. She drove me crazy."

"Why did you tell me this? This is more than I want to know."

"Guess what she had put in?"

"I can't imagine. Do I really have to know?"

"Hearts with diamonds in the middle."

"You could have spared me that," I answered. "I could have lived without that knowledge."

A Memory, The Drive-In Theatre

I WAS THIRTEEN YEARS OLD WHEN THE FIRST DRIVE-IN THEATRE came to Harrisburg, Illinois, and, because I was the luckiest girl in the world, my best friend's father owned it. Her name was Connie Beth Ingram and she was tall and had short blond hair and was the athletic type. I was redheaded and thick in the waist and had to get by on my personality and my ability to write book reports at a moment's notice for anyone who needed one.

Connie and I were devoted to each other. We never plotted behind each other's backs or got jealous of each other. We were friends and we lived in a small town at a time when the United States was recovering from a war and beginning to make its way back into full-blown democratic capitalism. For most of the years of my and Connie's lives our families had lived careful, rational lives with not much stuff or money. Now, like many families in the years after the war, our fathers were beginning to "make money." It was an exciting time. People in the United States hadn't started spending money yet. They were just getting back to work making it.

Mr. Ingram's construction of a drive-in theatre on his farmland was just such a project. It was built on a long, sloping hill with a huge raised screen at the bottom where a line of trees bordered a small creek. Spread out around the screen like a Greek amphitheatre were the parking places for cars and trucks. Beside each place was a tall metal post with a speaker waiting to be lifted out and attached to the driver's-side window. There was a gravel road leading from the highway past an admissions booth and on up to a concrete building that housed the projector and the concession stand.

The theatre opened just as summer began. Because I was Connie's friend, at least twice a week I was invited to spend the night and help with the drive-in. I would walk the two miles to her house outside of town. When I got there we would go with her mother to open the concession stand. For the first months of that summer Mr. and Mrs. Ingram were still "getting the kinks out" of the business and there was plenty to do. Usually Mr. Ingram ran the projector and Mrs. Ingram ran the concession stand but sometimes there would be problems with the speakers or a fight would start or people would be caught trying to sneak in and then Mrs. Ingram would take over the projector while Mr. Ingram solved the problem. When that happened Connie Beth was put in charge of the concession stand. Only thirteen years old and already she was the capable businesswoman she would later become.

I got to help! I got to fill sacks with popcorn and hand over candy bars and open Cokes and make change. I liked working in the concession stand more than I liked watching the movies. I liked it a lot better than sitting in a car with other people having to be quiet while the movie was on. I was not the type to sit quietly in a car while all around me the hot summer night was full of mystery and exciting people. If I was working in the concession stand I got to see everyone who came to the movie. I got to talk all I wanted and eat handfuls of popcorn when there was a lull and be the one who squirted hot butter onto the already luscious popcorn. I still like to make popcorn for people and I still make it in a pan and melt real butter to pour over it.

Mr. Ingram tried to pay me for working but I would never take his money. How could anyone need to be paid for being out in a field at night with the air full of the sounds of Warner Brothers or Metro-Goldwyn-Mayer and the sounds of pickup trucks bringing good-looking high school boys to buy buttered popcorn and Hershey bars and Coca-Colas? How could anyone want to be paid for being able to stand outside the concession stand and watch the stream of light coming out of the projector and running down the hill like a river to the edge of the woods where it became Lana Turner or Clark Gable or Elizabeth Taylor or Van Johnson or Henry Fonda?

Above us the stars were brilliant in a clear, black summer sky. On the screen human stars twinkled in their Hollywood perfection. In the cars and pickups high school kids kissed and ate popcorn. In the backs of pickups little kids sat with their grandmothers on lawn chairs and ate cookies they brought from home.

I stood beside the concession stand and watched it all. I was the luckiest girl in the world, I decided, to live in the modern world and be best friends with the daughter of the man who brought drive-in theatre to Harrisburg, Illinois. I was right.

Summer, A Memory

THE GREATEST SUMMERS OF MY LIFE WERE THE ONES I SPENT with my widowed grandmothers. One of them was soft and sweet and lived in the Mississippi delta. I pretty much had my way with her as she was recently widowed and was too worried and too busy running the plantation to overpower me physically or psychologically.

At least once every visit she would decide to spank me with her hairbrush but in the first place she couldn't catch me and in the second place she was so small and her inability to be mean so deep that if I decided to let her catch me and put me across her knees all she did was administer a few small taps to my derriere, breathing heavily and sighing the whole time. It was nice to be close to her and smell her bath powder but it did little to alter my behavior or improve my manners.

I called this grandmother Dan-Dan. I loved her dearly and named all my dogs after her for years. They were a series of fox terriers that came by train from her plantation to where I lived. I would name them Danny, overfeed them terribly and weep uncontrollably when they were run over by cars, as they all eventually were since it is against my nature to keep animals penned up behind fences.

My other grandmother was another matter. Her grandfather had been the governor of Mississippi and she had been sent to college at a time when almost no women were educated. She refused to marry until she was twenty-six, an unheard-of thing in those days. She met my grandfather at a house party in Natchez and married him the next week in a historic house called Dunleith.

Then she left Mississippi and went to live with him in Courtland, Alabama, a town his Scots family had built in north Alabama in the seventeen hundreds. It was barely a town. It was seven plantations that circled a square with a drugstore, a jail, a buggy store, and a picture show.

She had three sons, the oldest of whom was my father, and she liked boys better than she liked girls and was quick to say so. I treated her accordingly. "I like going to Mississippi to see Dan-Dan better than I like coming to see you," I told her many times. Grannie Gilchrist and I did not mince words or pretend to like each other more than we did.

Still, there were reasons for visiting her that made me want to keep returning. To tell the truth I could not stay away from the woman. The fact that you had to earn her love was a magnet, and, at least once each summer, I would pack my bags and go and visit her. We always visited Grannie one child at a time. She did not want a house full of rowdy children as my grandmother in Mississippi did. She wanted to do her duty by letting us visit when our parents needed to get rid of one of us, and I'm sure she welcomed the opportunity to correct some of the child-rearing faults her disapproved-of daughters-in-law were committing, but, especially where little girls were concerned, she wanted one child at a time and on her own terms.

I was always glad to leave, but I was always eager to go again the next summer. For one thing she had the most books of any person I had ever known. Every room in her house was full of books. Almost every wall had bookshelves from floor to ceiling filled with wonderful books. I was an inveterate reader. I read four or five library books every week, but Grannie's house was better than a library. For one thing, there was no adult section. Anything that was there you could read, because if a book was in that house, she had read it and if there was anything in it that could corrupt a child or lead them into evil she had thrown it away and written the publisher to complain.

Meals were easy at Grannie's house. She subsisted on toasted biscuits, pound cake and tea, and if I wanted to I could live on that too. If I wanted poached eggs or chicken I could have it but she didn't force food on me or ever try to make me eat vegetables. She ate to live. Food was way down on the scale of things that interested her. That was right in my line of thinking. All I ever wanted from food was enough sugar to keep on reading.

We read all day, on daybeds made up with sparkling white bedspreads, on sofas covered with muslin slipcovers, on porch swings and in rockers and lying on the floor on handmade rugs she bought from people who made them for a living. Grannie almost never bought anything unless by doing so she was helping the salesperson. She was as far from a materialist as it is possible to be. Stuff did not interest her. Bauhaus would have loved her closet, which contained six shirtwaist dresses, three for summer and three for winter, two pairs of high-topped shoes, several cardigan sweaters, and a wool coat.

The rooms in her house were airy and plain and cool. There was a wide porch across the front of the house and in the front yard a massive live oak tree with an incredible treehouse. When I was six years old her sons had given her money to have her bathrooms modernized. She had not asked for the money and tried to refuse it but when they insisted and put it in her bank account she accepted it and thanked them. Then she called a carpenter and had him build her a copy of a treehouse she had played in as a child. It was in the front yard of Jefferson Davis's house in Biloxi, Mississippi. "I have always wanted one of those treehouses," she told my father and his brothers. "And I like my bathrooms as they are."

So, by the time I was visiting her, there was this magnificent treehouse with a staircase worthy of a mansion. The stairs led to a circular porch with a beautiful white railing. There was a bench around the center of the tree and a table and chairs to match the railing.

Grannie and her closest friends would go up there in the afternoons and have tea. Grannie would fix the tea herself, put it on a silver tray and carry it up the stairs. Aunt Mamie would be behind her carrying a second tray with cups and saucers and linen napkins. Carey Hotchkiss and Mrs. Tweedy would already be in the tree setting the table and putting out cookies and beaten biscuits. Ellen Martin was already having trouble with her hip when the treehouse was new so I don't remember her ever carrying anything heavier than a tin of cheese straws.

The ladies would settle down in their chairs. Grannie would pour the tea. Conversation would begin. Civilization was being served.

Most of Grannie's friends dressed in versions of the shirtwaist dresses she favored but Grannie's were always solid colors or small pale stripes. Some of the other ladies were bolder and wore flowered prints or lace-trimmed blouses and dark skirts. They wore sensible shoes, black for fall and winter, white for spring and summer. They talked of books and weddings and sermons, of trips their progeny were taking or had just returned from taking. They shared letters from distant cousins or people who had moved away. They did not say mean things about other people and they did not dwell on bad news. If there was bad news from somewhere they delivered it quickly and moved on to better topics. A person who gossiped or said mean things would not have been welcome in that treehouse.

By the time I was nine or ten Ellen Martin's hip problems had progressed to the point where she could no longer climb the stairs. When this happened the ladies moved the tea parties to the front porch. They would not have dreamed of flaunting their superior mobility by going up the stairs when their friend could not.

Mrs. Martin was one of the two women for whom I am named. Her name was Ellen Gilchrist Martin and she was the mother of my father's favorite cousin. My father swore I was named for this woman but my mother said I was named for *her* great-grandmother, Ellen Connell Martin Biggs Taylor (she outlived three husbands and died at ninety-eight), who lived until I was four years old and whom I can remember. I have always sided with my mother in this controversy as I would rather be named for my great-great-grandmother than for a cousin.

My middle name is Louise, for Grannie, but this did not make her like me anymore or stop thinking I was a bad child who needed taking in hand.

One thing that annoyed her year after year was that my mother would send me down there with suitcases full of starched and

ironed dress-up dresses. I would wear several of them a day, changing clothes as the mood suited me and throwing the dirty ones on
the floor. I would climb trees and sit in the treehouse in white pique
dresses or pink linen dresses or whatever suited my fancy.

One summer, when I was there for a month while my brother had
his eye operated on, she sent for a seamstress to make me some practical seersucker playsuits. They were a child's version of the shirtwaist
dresses in which she lived her life. I hated them and would not put
them on until finally she wore me down by telling me how hard the
seamstress had worked to make them and how sad the seamstress's
life was and how disappointed she was going to be if she found out I
didn't like the things she had struggled so hard to make for me.

Shades of The Poor Little Match Girl, a story she had read to me
when I was learning how to read. Yes, I would wear the playsuits, I
decided. I would not be the mean person who added to the store of a
poor seamstress's troubles. Besides, by then I had realized how much
easier it was to climb trees in playsuits than in starched dresses. Also,
I had decided the playsuits made me look like Jane in the Tarzan
books, which had influenced me so much the year before that I had
gone to the refrigerator and gotten out some raw meat and tried to eat
it. When Tarzan and his friends made a kill in the forest they always
took the raw meat in their hands and devoured it hungrily, savoring
the hot, bloody taste. The meat I got from our refrigerator was neither hot nor bloody, and I knew I would never be a huntress if that
was the reward.

After I settled into my seersucker playsuit mode I played Tarzan
for days. Sometimes I was Jane, in my full playsuit, fixing lunch for
Tarzan on magnolia leaves with mimosa blossoms in my hair. Sometimes I was Tarzan himself, with my halter pulled down around my
waist so I could beat on my chest to call my elephants in emergencies. Sometimes my cousin Sykes was there and I would let him be
Tarzan while I was either Jane or a band of chimpanzees or mountain apes.

Sykes was the grandson of Ellen Martin, for whom I was either
named or not named, and he was a perfect companion. He was a

year younger than I was and he was an only child. It has been my experience that only children make wonderful friends. Perhaps this is because they are not in the habit of fighting for power like children with close siblings. Perhaps it is because they are hungry for play-mates and work harder to be pleasant.

Sykes was game for anything I thought up to do, even though he was watched very closely by his mother and grandmother and for-bidden to do anything that was dangerous. His grandmother lived in horror he would be hurt and would have lectured him to within an inch of him losing his hearing if she had found out half the things we found to do in Courtland, Alabama.

We climbed to the top of a lookout tower, which was forbidden. We swam in a cow pond. Completely forbidden. We climbed to the top of a sixty-foot-tall magnolia tree in front of the Courtland Presby-terian Church. Not exactly forbidden since they had forgotten to tell us not to do that.

Unless you have spent time climbing magnolia trees you might not know that their trunks are covered with a thick black pitch only Clo-rox bleach will remove from clothes. It would have made sense if our grandmothers got mad about that but they did not. They were just, and would not scold us for something they had forgotten to forbid.

My grandmother was fierce but she was not indomitable. Some-times she would tire of overseeing me and would send me out into the country to visit plantations run by younger, stronger cousins. My favorite was a plantation where the father drank and the mother had four small children. I could do anything I liked out there but I was never allowed to spend the night. I wanted very much to spend the night out there. I had heard the father got so drunk one night he climbed into a baby bed by mistake and slept there. I wanted to be there if it happened again. I had never seen a person get drunk and I was curious about it.

A place I was allowed to visit any time I wanted was my Great-Un-cle George's house, which was a block from my grandmother's. It was a large, square, white mansion sitting in the middle of two acres of untended weeds and pecan trees. I would dress in nice clothes and walk over there to visit Uncle George and Aunt Suzy and go down in their storm cellar to look at the canned goods.

The mansion contained every newspaper and piece of string and rubber band that had ever been delivered there, plus every box and jar and magazine. By the time I was visiting there was almost no place left to sit down but Uncle George and Aunt Suzy would scurry around rearranging stacks of newspapers and find a place for me. We would talk about things for awhile. I would tell them everything that was going on, in Harrisburg, Illinois, where I lived, and out at Summerwood where Sykes lived and also plots of movies I had seen or books I had read. Then Uncle George would straighten his tie and put on his seersucker jacket and his hat and we would walk to town to get ice cream cones. We would eat them as we walked back towards the mansion across the stubble-covered field that was Uncle George's yard. It was hard to keep up a conversation and also keep the ice cream from running down my hand but I could do it. For his part, Uncle George, who was in his seventies and at least six feet four inches tall, never spilled a drop on his coat or tie. When we got back to the mansion we would go into the living room and I would help Uncle George and Aunt Suzy move the sofa and the Indian rug and open the trap door that led to the cellar. We would go down a set of wooden stairs into a long tunnel with wooden supports and shelves cut into earthen walls. The shelves were filled with canned goods as old as many of the newspapers in the house. It was comforting to know we had a place to go in case of a tornado or domestic war. I took this as one more example of the riches of my family.

The summer I was twelve I brought my best friend, Cynthia Hancock, to Courtland with me. She was the prettiest girl in our school and could tap dance and twirl batons and play the piano and choreograph dance routines, among other talents. She was the most popular girl in Harrisburg and being her best friend was a surefire way to be elected cheerleader and never run out of boyfriends, as the ones she tired of always turned to me for sympathy.

Everyone in Courtland fell in love with her. Not only Sykes but my older cousins too, boys who had paid scant attention to me until I showed up with Cynthia by my side.

Grannie loved Cynthia and approved of her, as she was quiet and polite and acted the way Grannie thought young ladies were supposed to act. So Grannie didn't object when Cynthia and I decided to set up headquarters in her attic.

Grannie had a superb attic. During the Second World War, when Courtland was the site of an Air Corps Training Base, the attic had been floored and turned into an apartment for a pilot and his wife. There was still an alcove with two large fans and a dresser and an iron bed covered with a pretty chenille bedspread. The attic had an exotic feel, as if it had never lost the excitement and dark romance of aviation and young marriage and war.

We dusted the place and swept the floor and washed and dried the gauzy curtains in the dormer window that looked out upon the treehouse. At night, when Grannie was in bed reading Scottish histories, we would lie on the bed sipping the crème de menthe we found in the dresser and pretend we were movie stars or beautiful young women with pilots for boyfriends.

Cynthia was fascinated by the flowers or gardenias to put on the dresser. Later, when we were getting ready to be driven home, she made a collection of all the local flowers. We wrapped the stems in wet cotton and nursed them all the way home to Harrisburg, a twelve-hour car trip in those days.

My fifteen-year-old cousin, Quart McWhorter, had a driver's license and Grannie would let us get in the car with him at night and drive to the closed filling station to get Cokes out of the Coke machine. We would drive around town with the windows down and then out to the abandoned air force base to drive up and down the runways in the moonlight. An even older cousin, Bobby Tweedy, age sixteen, was also allowed to take us riding in his car, since his grandmother was one of the afternoon tea drinkers.

Cynthia's presence was opening doors for me in Courtland. Now, not only was it a place where I read books, it was becoming a place where we could act them out. Who loved Cynthia? Who did Cynthia love? How far away in kin do you have to be to love someone? This was an important issue as I was related to everyone in town and if all cousins were verboten I would be left out of love. I finally decided that Bobby Tweedy was the only one far enough away in kinship to guarantee my children would not be blind if I married him. So I decided to love Bobby. There was no danger that he would love me back so it was a perfect romance. A love affair I completely made up was a love affair I could control.

All things being equal I would probably have rather loved Sykes, for his blond hair and unfailing good nature and ability to stand up to his grandmother but Bobby Tweedy was also very handsome and had the added virtue of being able to shake a Coca-Cola until it spewed a fountain ten feet in the air.

"Oh, Bobby, Bobby," I would say to Cynthia as we cuddled down in the iron bed to go to sleep. "I have to tell you that I love you. I do. I really do. I have to admit it."

"Oh, Sykes, Sykes, oh, Quart," she would answer. "I love you too. I think we should get married and have children."

Then we would dissolve in laughter, laughing so hard we almost fell off the bed. How did we know it was funny? How did we know romantic love was so absolutely funny?

Grannie seemed to stop worrying about me the summer Cynthia was there. I guess she thought Cynthia would keep an eye on me, or else, perhaps a new Thomas Costain novel had come in the mail and she was too caught up in the plot to care.

As I got older Grannie and I became better friends. Maybe I had taught her to like girls after all. Or maybe, just maybe, she had recognized traits in me that could only have come from her gene pool. Later in my life I met and knew the grandchildren of her sisters and they became true soul mates among my huge store of cousins. They are mostly bookish, bossy women who married *Newsweek* editors or became Episcopal lay readers or early civil rights workers or architects or anything else they could think up to do to dominate and challenge, to civilize and question.

Because my grandmothers were so wonderful to me I have always loved being a grandmother. The first grandchild, whose mother was my close friend, has always been as close to me as my own child. His mother and father let me have him whenever I wanted him for as long as I wanted him to stay. He had a tent in the center of my living room and a permanent place in the center of my heart. His two sisters are also very, very close to me. I have not had the constant access to the remaining thirteen children or the great-grandchildren but the way I feel about them is so powerful they feel it and respond to it.

I have tried to make memories for them as wonderful as the ones my grandparents made for me but there is no longer a world where children can come and spend the summer in their grandparents' homes.

A Home in the Highland

Keeping Houses

———————⟨◦⟩———————

I LIVE IN TWO PLACES, AND I LOVE THEM BOTH. MY MAIN HOME is in Fayetteville, Arkansas, a college town in the Ozark Mountains. I live on the highest hill in a quiet cul-de-sac, surrounded by friends. When I'm there, I am content to be an adult and talk to other adults and teach graduate students two days a week at the University of Arkansas.

I love Fayetteville. I like hills and vistas and hardworking people and fighting snow in winter and chiggers in the summer. You have to be tough to live in Fayetteville at certain times of the year. January and February and parts of March are bitterly cold and seem to last forever. It doesn't help that I live in a house built by a famous architect who was a student of Frank Lloyd Wright's and built my house the summer he came home from Taliesin West. The floors are made of stone and scored concrete. The walls are glass. It is so cold in this house in winter I think I must be a lunatic to stay. Yet I do stay because it's beautiful. Jones disliked putting gutters on his houses, so the pitched roofs make wonderful icicles that hang down outside. Light comes in the windows and the skylights, and you might as well be sleeping in a tent you are so close to nature.

I never meant to be here in the winter, but then I started teaching, and I love the students, so I can't leave. Besides, I get a lot of work done when I'm snowed in. No chiggers, no pollen, and never a dull moment trying to outwit an E. Fay Jones house and stay warm: my main line of defense is heated mattress pads and UGG boots. It used to be heated blankets, but the hippies say heated blankets cause cancer so I switched to heated mattress pads.

My other home is a small condominium on a beach in Ocean Springs, Mississippi. I bought it in 1995 to be near my three eldest grandchildren when they were growing up. I wanted to be there to drive the girls to dancing lessons and watch my grandson play baseball and basketball. I had seen my own sons grow up. I know how fast it happens. If you aren't there to watch it, you don't get a second chance.

It is a twelve-hour drive from Fayetteville to the Mississippi coast: I start off going due north and downhill. By the time I am forty miles down the mountains, it's warmer. By the time I get to my brother's house in Jackson, Mississippi, where my family has a long history, I can take off my boots and put on pretty shoes. I usually spend the night in Jackson, where I see my nieces and nephews and my mother's antique furniture, which my sister-in-law lets my brother keep, wall to wall, in every room. My childhood is in my brother's house, and I like to visit there and be reminded. I usually stay until noon, then drive the last four hours to Ocean Springs.

My sparsely furnished three-bedroom condominium is waiting for me there, looking and feeling just like home. The condo is a no-worries house. Even on cold days, it's as warm as toast. "So this is how normal people live," I'm always thinking. "They are nice and warm and don't have to wear boots inside their houses."

I take a deep breath, carry my clothes upstairs, and take the sign off my typewriter that says, "Do not touch this machine. This is how grandmother makes a living."

The Mississippi coast is not like south Florida, but it always seems warm enough for sandals and short-sleeved shirts, except for now and then. In Ocean Springs, I take long walks on the beach every morning, watch sunsets on the pier, and wait for various offspring to come visit. It's wonderful to have a refrigerator full of whole milk and chocolate pudding. I even buy juice boxes. I like to see them sitting there, just the right size for certain little girls and boys, something they can handle. I especially like the little straws that are attached to the boxes.

When I am in Ocean Springs, I have many grandchildren and great-grandchildren within reach. They are not as easy to handle as adults, but they have nonstop energy and imagination and never have to go to the doctor for colonoscopies or skin cancer checks, or get prescription drugs for sleeplessness. Children live in the present, and since I am trying to learn to do that, they are my favorite companions in my old age. I like to watch children sleep. You can walk around a room and take things out of drawers and it does not awaken them. Children sleep in a state of grace. I have much to learn from them before I get any deeper into my seventies (now eighties).

My condominium complex is the only thing on Ocean Springs's two beaches that survived Hurricane Katrina. The contents of the lower floors were swept out to sea by a forty-foot wave, but the structures were sound when the wave receded. Thanks to the smart people who serve on the condominium board, we were well insured when it came time to rebuild and repair. In September 2007, I moved back into my condo and went to work spending all my money to fill it back up with furniture and beds and toys. I refuse to let my grandchildren think a once-in-a-lifetime storm can ruin all our fun.

If I were younger, I might have sold the place, but my older grandchildren lost their childhood home in the storm and need a place to stay when they come home for weddings and festivals and to see their friends. Besides, I love Ocean Springs as much as I love Fayetteville. I like to walk on the beach and marvel at the flatness of the land, and watch the sun rise and fall on the Gulf of Mexico. Since the hurricane, I like to look out at the sea and think about all the silver and china and lamps and furniture and coffeepots and toys and bicycles that were swept out to sea. All the old letter jackets and cheerleading costumes and dance recital props and leaf blowers and automobiles. The red electric truck I bought for the children to drive to the beach, and then drive home and inside through the sliding glass doors, is out there somewhere, rusted now, perhaps a home for squid or barracuda.

The children and I were planning on buying a new truck, but while I was in Fayetteville the builder put on new doors, and they're too narrow to drive a truck through. Maybe we'll build a toy garage.

I am a lucky woman. I have two homes that wrap around me and make me feel safe. Fayetteville, beautiful little wooded town. Nothing to do but teach school and write books and wait for the mail. Ocean Springs, children and toys and a typewriter that is mostly turned to the wall. Moist air that fills in my wrinkles and curls my hair. No worries, no freezing, no shoes.

Update: We found an electric green truck at a garage sale. It only cost twenty-five dollars and isn't as dependable as the red Chevrolet Silverado but it is *a lot faster*, once it starts.

We leave it outside or squeeze it in the front door.

Note: If you are under fifty years old you must remember that this took place "a long, long time ago in another galaxy," a world where it was taken for granted that men went to work and women stayed home and decorated the house and taught manners to the children.

How I Learned to Love and Trust Women, Since, After All, I Am One

IN 1984 I WAS LIVING IN FAYETTEVILLE, ARKANSAS, WRITING books and managing my own money for the first time in my life. I was recently divorced. Until then my financial life had been handled by my father and my husbands. There had been three husbands but I never took money or alimony from any of them. My brother had been investing my money in U.S. Treasury bills which were paying an unheard-of dividend of twelve percent. He had been doing this for a year and had recently decided I should learn to do it for myself. He set me up with an account executive at Merrill Lynch in Fayetteville. I almost never saw the man and can't remember his name.

Then one day, the man called me up and said he was leaving Merrill Lynch and had turned my account over to another broker. He made an appointment for me to meet the broker at 11:30 the following Monday.

I dressed up in my best clothes and went down to the firm at the appointed time. The receptionist took my name. A moment later a beautiful, tall redheaded woman came through the door. She had clear brown eyes and the most intelligent face I had seen in years.

She said her name was Sue Plattner and she was going to be my stockbroker. "Oh, no," I said. "I don't want a woman to handle my money. I don't think I could do that."

I had never known a woman who handled money or did anything important in the business world. I was the only girl in my family. I had two brothers, four uncles, and ten male first cousins. They were physicians and pilots and federal court judges and lawyers and bankers and engineers and naval offices and all sorts of proud, wonderful things in the big world. The also beautiful and well-educated and intelligent women of my childhood worked behind the scenes. They were nurses and secretaries and accountants and maids and nursemaids and cooks and assistant editors and court reporters. It was understood by all intelligent people that women were doing more than their share of the work, not to mention giving psychological support to the men, but they didn't have the positions of responsibility. They made budgets for homes and businesses but they didn't make investments in the stock market.

"Let's go to lunch," Sue Plattner said. "I'll tell you about myself. Maybe you will change your mind."

Sue is twenty years younger than I am. She had gone to the University of Arkansas and been on the Pan-Hellenic Council, which is the governing board of the large sorority system at big public colleges. This is a position of responsibility and power and we talked about the work she had done there to keep young women from drinking alcohol and taking drugs.

I had never met a woman who did something as dangerous and exciting as help people manage their money.

While we ate she began to tell me about what she could do to help me. She talked to me about what investing should be. (Like a good teacher's daughter she was teaching me.) She told me what the stock market is, what treasury bonds are, what sort of things are possible in long-term investing, what she wanted for her customers. She explained risk and diversification, municipal bonds, dividends, inflation, things I had never really understood. I knew the words but I didn't understand the concepts. Until that luncheon I had just put my faith in men wearing suits and let it go at that.

Sue and I went back to the Merrill Lynch office, where she got out a folder with a list of my investments and we went over them one by one. She showed me a twenty-year chart of treasury bonds and explained why they might not always be paying twelve percent. She suggested we put some of the money into longer-term bonds and maybe buy a few mutual funds while the stock market was down. I stayed in Sue's office for several hours as she taught me things and we made plans.

I went home dazzled. As Sue Plattner's ideas and suggestions started to make money for me, I began to look at my prejudices with a sharp eye. *I am a woman,* I told myself. *I think I'm smarter than my brothers. I know I'm meaner than they are if I have to be. Why do I think someone like me won't be as good as a man at anything? Hell's bells, as my mother would say. I made that money. Why would I think someone like me wasn't good enough to handle it?*

Shortly after meeting Sue I hired a woman to be my CPA. Her name was Betty. We made tea and talked awhile.

Then we got out my messy papers and began to try to figure out how much money I had made and how many deductions I had.

"Where are your receipts?" she asked.

"I don't have any," I answered. "I didn't know I needed them."

The next day she came back to my house and gave me a pair of notebooks with plastic pockets in the covers so I could begin to keep track of my cash expenses.

"An artist or writer can deduct CDs, going to the movies, visiting museums, buying books," she told me. "This is going to be fun."

It was fun. Me and my CPA against the mean-spirited, greedy "feds." She taught me about the ever-changing, absurdly complicated tax code. Every winter we fought the tax battle together. It was a strong bond between us.

I began looking for a woman doctor, but that took awhile because they were hard to find twenty years ago. I had to wait until the daughter of a friend finished medical school and came home to practice to have the pleasure of a woman doctor.

By the time my literary agent retired a few years later it was easy for me to switch to a woman in his office. It never occurred to me to think she was a woman and he had been a man. I had become accustomed to women in powerful positions and aware of how good they are at everything they do. They are funny, charming, energetic, ambitious, fabulously *dependable* and just plain old good.

I don't want to trade one set of prejudices for another; still I can't help but note the advantages of working with another woman. If they are good at what they do you end up being friends.

I remember another lunch date with Sue Plattner a few years after we met. She came running into the restaurant apologizing for being late. She had just been given the results of a test that showed she was carrying triplets. She went right on working while bringing those three beautiful boys into the world. They are identical twin redheaded boys and a gorgeous black-haired baby who looks like his Italian father.

Later, Sue and her older son, Adam, drove down to Jackson, Mississippi, to meet and talk with my powerful old father. It was his shadow she was fighting as she tried to keep me from thinking the markets were going to collapse and we should all be in gold.

I still love men. I understand them and I like to watch them operate. They work from a different set of drives and hormones than women do. But it's peaceful to do business with women. I like being able to gossip about our families while I'm getting a physical exam.

I didn't understand it as it happened, but my life has been following, sometimes slowly and sometimes in great surges, the changes in this amazing culture in which we live.

I rejected the wild fringes of feminism, but I cried when I read in a book by Germaine Greer that women didn't have to give up their last names when they marry. Thanks to three husbands I had been Ellen Walker, then Ellen Bloodworth, then Ellen Walker again, then Ellen Kullman.

On the day I read that line in Greer's book I walked into the dining room and sat down at the table and wrote my name on a piece of paper. Ellen Gilchrist. Then I cried. I have been Ellen Gilchrist ever since. I like my name even if it is hard to spell and even though my radical friends like to remind me it came from my father.

Fall 2004, The Origin of Ball Games

LEST WE FORGET WHERE WE CAME FROM. I HAVE BEEN PLAYING a game with the squirrels and chipmunks in my backyard. The game began in July, when, after a year of perfect weather for plants and trees, my hickory trees produced a record-setting number of hickory nuts. When the nuts begin to grow the squirrels start gathering. Squirrels who live on the many oak and maple trees on my acre of land and in neighboring yards all begin to spend time on my roof where the overhanging hickory branches make a convenient grocery store for them. Immature hickory nuts are not edible even for ravenous squirrels and chipmunks but that does not stop them from tearing them down with their paws and teeth and taking a bite and dropping the rest on my long concrete back porch. It's only a minor addiction at this point, although my game and fish commissioner friend says squirrels love the smell and taste of hickory nuts better than anything in the world. When I see them tearing into the immature nuts I am always reminded of Richard Brautigan's wonderful crazy books that contained recipes for things like hickory nut soup.

Back to the squirrels. Every year when the hickory nuts begin to ripen the squirrels arrive in force and eat them all day long and drop enormous amounts of trash on the porch and come down onto the porch and eat nuts on the stone wall that supports the porch and when they are finished with the nuts they climb back up on the roof and chew on the California redwood trim of this beautiful Fay Jones house that I was lucky enough to buy when it was a wreck and very cheap because Fay was a year away from winning the gold medal of the American Institute of Architects.

When this happens I get mean. I call the fish and game man and he comes and traps them and carries them off to his property and turns them loose in a stand of wild pecan trees. Sometimes he catches a few possums by accident but we just turn them loose on the back lot. It is sad to see the house-eating squirrels' dismay when they are in the traps and waiting to be transported to greener fields but when they begin to tear up the house I feel justified.

I could end all this by having the trees sprayed with poison to keep them from producing nuts but the poison is so toxic only a few old tree men from out in the country will agree to spray it on trees and I can't bring myself to add poison to the lovely little ecosystem in my yard.

So, this year, with the bumper crop of hickory nuts, I have devised a plan that seems to me fair and Zen. I was planning on being home most of the summer and fall anyway so I started going out in the early morning and late afternoon and collecting all the nuts that fall on the porch and wall and taking them down the hill and putting them near a creek bed. I am trying to train the squirrels to have their addictive hickory nut feasts in another location.

Another trick I am using is to have my twelve-year-old neighbor, John Tucker McCormick, come over in his spare time from his baseball and football careers and throw the nuts one at a time all the way down to the bottom of my lot into an area behind my trampoline. While he's here he sweeps off the trampoline and jumps on it awhile to make sure it hasn't rotted and become an attractive nuisance.

All of this has helped and I am getting very long and thin in the waist from having bent over and picked up somewhere in the vicinity of six thousand hickory nuts or maybe six million. It is amazing how many nuts two large hickory trees can produce given perfect weather and plenty of rain for a year.

Only once or twice have I caught squirrels eating on the redwood trim and they have been doing it on the back of the house where I never have to look at the damage.

~ ~ ~

This morning I was playing a new game. Instead of bending over to pick up the nuts or sweeping them into a dustpan I began to kick them into a pile. Then I began to try to kick them into the dustpan. Soccer, I thought, dodging a nut that was falling from the roof where an early morning addict was picking the last of the nuts and dropping half of them in his frenzy. I have been hit once or twice this month as the nut falls have become greater.

Every day I think, "My God, this has to be the last of the nuts. How many nuts can two trees bear?" But it is never the last.

I wonder if you could eat these things, I keep thinking, and, poor little squirrels and chipmunks, maybe I shouldn't make them use their calories going all the way to the creek for breakfast. Still, there are plenty on the other side of the porch. All the ones that fall on the ground are theirs. All the ones that fall on my porch get moved. They are going to move their little hungry derrieres away from my redwood trim, if it's the last thing I ever accomplish in my short but happy life on the planet earth. Ninety thousand years until the next ice age.

I should learn to love the squirrels as much as I love the chipmunks, but I can't. I should be perfect but I'm not. I should keep on trying to be a Zen person and I will. *The Pill Versus the Springhill Mine Disaster* and *All Watched Over by Machines of Loving Care* and *The Abortion* are some of the wonderful and increasingly forgotten books by the City Lights poet named Richard Brautigan. *The Abortion* is about a library up in New England where people go to turn in books instead of take them out. Anytime anyone writes a book they can go up there and put their book in. This is so much more Zen than going through the process of publication and peer review and book signings and so forth. Somewhere in the middle of the book there is an abortion, but it's not very important. I can't remember now if the abortion happens or just almost happens.

I learned so much from Richard Brautigan. I learned to have fun with writing. I learned to put photographs and paintings of my friends on the covers of my books. I learned to have real titles instead of boring ones and I learned how to describe behavior from a short story called "The Koolaid Wino."

Thanks to those squirrels and to the wonderful, almost forgotten poet and writer Richard Brautigan, I am having a divine and productive morning to make up for the fact that two of my friends have died in the last month and another has been diagnosed with a terrible cancer.

We must press on. Ninety thousand years to go, although I have a theory that if we can keep from blowing ourselves up with it, we can use nuclear energy to melt ice when the next ice age starts.

From left: Juliet Jane Walker, Josephine Elean Walker, Ellen Gilchrist at Josephine's christening, Trinity Episcopal Church, New Orleans, 2012.

Back row: Pierre Gautier Walker IV, Abigail Walker, Ellen Gilchrist, Anastasia Campeau, Natalie DuBois, Cameron Walker; front row: Juliet Walker, Josephine Walker, Aurora Walker, Ellen Gilchrist Walker Perkins, Felicia Walker. Grandchildren and son at Josephine's christening at Trinity Episcopal Church, 2012.

Marshall Kingman Walker and
Ellen Gilchrist, 1986, Fayetteville,
Arkansas, my oldest grandson. A life-
changing event for me.

Ellen Gilchrist, William
Garth Gilchrist, Jr. Gulf
Shores, Alabama, 1966.

Ellen Gilchrist, New Orleans, Louisiana. In front of my house on Webster Street. Photo taken by my husband, Frederick Sydney Kullman. The only print blouse I ever liked in my life. Wearing an old Timex watch I kept going for twenty-five years. I liked the leather band.

My mother, father, my younger brother, and I, at the wedding of my only girl first cousin, Nell Kleinschmidt Mabry, in summer, at the New Orleans Country Club. We had just been to Pierre's graduation from Country Day High School, 1979. From left, Aurora Louise Alford Gilchrist, William Garth Gilchrist, Jr., Robert Alford Gilchrist, Ellen Louise Gilchrist.

Ellen Gilchrist in a suite at the Ritz Hotel in Paris, 1978, where I lived on white wine, homemade potato chips, hot chocolate, and asparagus. My first trip to Europe. On my honeymoon with Frederick Sydney Kullman.

My family when I was Mrs. Marshall Peteet Walker. From left, Marshall Walker, Marshall Walker, Jr., Garth Gilchrist Walker, Pierre Gautier Walker IV, Ellen Louise Gilchrist Walker. It took me hours to get those little boys in all those shirts and ties. My mother was helping me dress them. My father had bought me that beautiful, pale gold wool suit. Kansas City, Missouri, 1964.

My freshman year in high school. I was the features editor on the high school newspaper. We were the school geniuses. I wrote all the school plays also. No one ever changed a word of anything I wrote. We never heard of the word edit.

My older brother, William Garth Gilchrist III. He died last year. He had an eidetic memory and was a fantastic athlete. He gave me unconditional love and protection every day of his life. I was jealous of his privileges but finally outgrew it and appreciated his amazing life.

Ellen Gilchrist in the sixth or seventh grade. The only time I ever had bangs. It was a last attempt to keep my hair out of my eyes since I never stop moving.

A wonderful two weeks in about 1943, in the middle of the Second World War. My mother's sister, Roberta Alford, was visiting us in Seymour, Indiana, where my father was building an airport for the United States Air Force. My pilot uncle had come home from Europe where he was flying bombing missions over Germany. My brother and I worshiped him and had photographs of the airplanes he flew all over our bedroom walls. From left: my older brother, William Garth Gilchrist III, Ellen Gilchrist, Lt. Colonel William David Gilchrist.

On side: my older brother, William Gilchrist (Dooley) and a friend named Ronnie. They were always armed; after all, we were at war with Germany and Japan. In foreground: my aunt, Roberta Alford, as usual trying desperately to get my crazy red hair out of my face. She could figure out ways to braid my very soft, thin, wavy hair because I liked her so much I'd stand still while she did it.

1943, Seymour, Indiana, September. From left: Ellen Gilchrist and a fox terrier puppy named Danny, after my maternal grandmother; Aurora Louise Alford Gilchrist, my mother; with my new brother Robert Alford Gilchrist.

Dooley (my older brother) and I on a usual Saturday morning. We rode real horses nearly every day but we also loved to play cowboys and Indians on stick horses. I was usually armed also but liked pistols better than rifles. The only clothes I really liked to wear were jodhpurs and coveralls. I needed pockets. I still do.

On the front porch of our house in Mound City, Illinois, where my father was chief engineer of the United States Corps of Engineers who were building levees at the confluence of the Ohio and Mississippi rivers. About 1939. My paternal grandmother, Louise Winchester Clark Gilchrist, was visiting us and we were all dressed up holding dolls. I liked to own dolls and put them in their beds to sleep but I preferred horses and guns or roller skates or stilts.

My mother, Aurora Louise Alford Gilchrist, and I in front of our house in Mound City, Illinois. We are dressed to go to church in matching outfits my mother had made on her footpedal sewing machine. She always smelled of wonderful perfume her family in the Mississippi delta would mail to her. Her blond hair was as thin and wispy as my red hair and she would work very hard to create ways to get it out of our faces.

Nearing the end of the Second World War. On the front porch of our house in Seymour, Indiana. From left: my brother William Garth Gilchrist III, my brother Robert Alford Gilchrist, and myself. I had gotten chubby from eating mayonnaise sandwiches and Mother had begun to make me outfits with long vests.

In front of my father's Corps of Engineers office on the main street of Mound City, Illinois, 1940. I carried notebooks and pencils everywhere as I had learned to read and write. The beautiful coat was a hand-me-down from Momma's beautiful young cousin Laura Finley, whose father was the only physician in three counties in the delta. She sent me fur coats and scarves and hats and all sorts of gorgeous clothes. I would wear anything if it had belonged to Laura Finley.

New Year's Day 2013 at the Pirates Park on Front Beach, Ocean Springs, Mississippi. Garrett Gilchrist Walker (great-grandson), Sean Daniel Walker (youngest grandson), and Ellen Gilchrist.

Diamonds, 2006

THE REASON TO WRITE IS TO LEARN. THE MORE I WRITE, THE
more I am forced to learn. This winter I am having to study geology
so that a teenage detective named Ingersol Manning can discover a
map to a kimberlite pipe in Berkeley, California. A kimberlite pipe
is the source of diamonds in the world. ". . . [A] relatively small hole
bored through the crust of the earth by an expanding combination of
carbon dioxide and water which rises from within the earth's mantle
and moves so fast driving magma to the surface that it breaks into the
atmosphere at supersonic speeds. Such events have occurred at ran-
dom through the history of the earth, and a kimberlite pipe could ex-
plode under Moscow next year. Rising so rapidly and from so deep a
source, a kimberlite pipe brings up exotic materials the like of which
could never appear in the shallow slow explosion of a Mount St. Hel-
ens or the flows of Mauna Loa. Among the materials are diamonds."*

A kimberlite pipe is about half a mile wide. If there is one underneath Ingersol's neighborhood, he and his friend Tammili, and their
mentor, the pianist Mrs. Coleman, will have to decide whether it's
worth telling anyone and having their neighborhood destroyed in the
process.

Anyway, I had to study geology for many nights. Two things happened because of that and both of them may prove to be irreversible.
First, I have begun to view the world from an entirely different per-
spective. I live in the Ozark Mountains, soft old hills left by glaciers
ten million years ago and since then eroded and worn down by rain

* John McPhee

117

and snow and forests. I have always thought they were beautiful and always been fascinated by the huge rocks that seem to spring up from the earth. Everywhere there are boulders of many sizes still working their way to the surface. My house is built of that rock, much of it broken up from larger stones.

Now I can no longer look around me and see the spring trees and the soft, new grasses and wildflowers. Now all I see is geomorphic time, the long processes that brought that rock down here from Canada.

The basins, ridges, shelves, gullies, erosions, roadcuts all have taken on huge, exciting lives. I am outside five hours a day exploring this and wondering and thinking. This is exciting work. This is an exciting life.

When I am through for the day I go to the bookstore and buy all the books on geology I can carry home. I have started giving them to children.

The reason I have become so excited about this subject is that I have found a use for it. If I can't see a practical use for something, sooner or later I get rid of it or give it away. I am using this geomorphic information to write a book that someday I might be able to sell, and that someday young people might read and be amused by, or learn something from. With that in mind I began my study of geology with enthusiasm. It has developed into a passion. I have not yet bought a rock hammer and a set of cold chisels but that will be next. I did almost have a wreck on a mountain road last Wednesday. I came to a roadcut with a great fall of granite. I must have passed that place hundreds of times as it is on the main road south from my home. "Granite," I screamed. "Granite, granite, granite." I threw on the brakes and was almost rear-ended by a highway patrol car. Fortunately, the officer had been maintaining a proper distance and was able to swerve around me. I was preparing a defense in my mind, but he drove on and did not bother me.

The second thing this new passion has done for me is to bring me back to consciousness after a long winter's sleep. Three weeks ago I was so bored I was watching television. While watching The Learning Channel I became convinced that there had been an Atlantis and that it was now Antarctica. I talked of nothing else for days, boring all my friends to death. While buying the geology books I picked up Carl Sagan's *The Demon-Haunted World*, and was brought back to consciousness about pseudoscience, even when it's on the Learning Channel. There may have been a city in the Aegean that toppled into the sea, or was covered by an earthquake, but that is a far cry from "the destruction of a continent on which had sprung forth a preternaturally advanced technical and mystical civilization."

The reason to write is to learn. The red streaks on rocks are iron. We are made of stardust, you, me, this newspaper, your thoughts, dreams, and hammers. Your diamond rings and number-two lead pencils. How blind we usually are. Not only to the real phenomena, which our five senses cannot see, but to the wonder that is here, beneath our feet, in Central Park, in every stone, the real history of the world, written in granite and marble and feldspar and dolomite and gypsum and opals and rubies and diamonds. Diamonds enter the earth's surface at Mach 2. How's that for a birth process?

My Paris and My Rome, Part I

I HAVE LOVED FAYETTEVILLE, ARKANSAS, SINCE THE FIRST TIME I drove there from New Orleans and found it waiting for me in all its autumn splendor. I had driven late the night before and spent the night in the small town of Morrillton, a hundred miles down the road. At dawn I bought a large cup of coffee at McDonald's and began the drive up into the Ozark Mountains. It was November, a clear, brilliant morning and the hills were covered with red and orange and violet and golden yellow leaves. Some mountains were covered with tall oak trees all turned a dark rich red. There were stretches of still-green bottomland, then hills of yellow and orange maples with red sumac climbing fences and abandoned barns and houses. I had not expected mountains or this spectacular autumn beauty.

Above the hills were brilliant blue skies with white cirrus clouds drifting past a full moon that stayed in view until late in the morning. The nearer I got to Fayetteville the steeper and more treacherous the road became. BEWARE, signs said. THIRTEEN PEOPLE KILLED HERE IN 1975. DON'T YOU BE NEXT.

It was exciting driving. You had to keep your hands on the wheel and your attention on the narrow curving road. I was hungry but there was no place to stop after I left the town of Alma, only this wild mountain road with its beautiful vistas and occasional pickup truck.

I was dressed in a designer suit with a ruffled white silk blouse. I was carrying a notebook containing one hundred and seventeen poems I had written the past summer and early fall. I had a CARTER FOR PRESIDENT button pinned to my suit jacket. I had picked it up the day before when I stopped in Jackson, Mississippi, to have lunch with Hodding Carter II and Patricia Derian, leading lights in the civil rights movement in Mississippi. They had insisted I stay the afternoon to hear Jimmy Carter speak at the Holiday Inn. I had never heard of Jimmy Carter and neither had anyone in Fayetteville when I got there. The poet Miller Williams, who later became a close friend of Carter's and edited his first book of poems, used to introduce me to visiting writers as the woman who brought the first Jimmy Carter button to town.

The reason I was making this 652-mile drive in my old Rambler station wagon was that I was "going to join the poets" in the Creative Writing Program at the University of Arkansas, where I now teach. My three wild, redheaded sons had joined the hippie rebellion of the 1970s. I had completely lost control of their lives. When they were born I had given up my ambitions to become a writer. I had transferred my energy and ambitions to my beautiful, tall sons. Now those sons had abandoned the paths I set for them and gone off to smoke marijuana with the hippies and do anything else they thought up to do.

"If my sons won't use the DNA, then I'll use it," I told my husband and my friends.

I called the writing program at the University of Arkansas and told them I was coming up there to learn how to publish books. "Come on," my old friend Jim Whitehead said. "I liked the poems you sent me. They are dangerous and powerful. You shouldn't be alone writing things like that."

I left my youngest son in New Orleans with my mother and my husband and got into my Rambler and started driving. I had no idea where I was going. I didn't look on a map until I crossed the Mississippi River into Arkansas. I certainly never imagined I was going to love the place as much as I did.

Fayetteville turned out to be much more beautiful and interesting and unique than I could have imagined, so free after the middle-class

life I was living in New Orleans, so open and funny and welcoming, full of exciting men and women doing things like building kilns
and designing houses and writing poetry and playing musical instruments and spending days floating down wild rivers in canoes, sleeping on blankets or in tents.

There was music everywhere. I took off my shoes and remembered how to dance. I had stopped drinking years before and I was
amazed to learn I could dance as well on Diet Coke as I had on gin
and vodka.

The poets welcomed me. I met a brilliant young poet named Frank
Stanford who asked if he could publish a book of my poems at Lost
Roads press. Yes, I said, and yes and yes and yes. The book was called
The Land Surveyor's Daughter.

A writer-professor named Bill Harrison talked me into trying my
hand at short stories. The second story I wrote for him won publication in the yearly magazine of the Associated Writing Programs and
gained me a lot of attention from publishers. So I wrote more stories
and Miller Williams published a book of them at the new University of Arkansas Press. The book sold ten thousand copies in a few
weeks. It has been reprinted many times by three publishers and also
in seven languages.

How could I not love Fayetteville after all it has given me? While I
was making my name in literature my youngest son left the hippies
and came to Fayetteville to get a degree in journalism and then a
doctorate from the law school. My oldest son left the hippies and
came here to get a degree in land surveying so he could support his
wife and child. My middle son stops off frequently in between trips
around the world as a ship's captain. He loves the air in Fayetteville.
He says it's a good place to breathe.

Over the years my oldest grandchildren have come here for weeks
in the summers to go to basketball and tennis and drama camps at
the university. An Olympic swimmer at the university taught them
to swim one summer. They still have extraordinarily good strokes.

When I see them swimming I remember the tall beautiful girl who charged me fifteen dollars an hour to teach them things they might never have learned anyplace else.

This town is magic. It has a magical quality for those of us who love it.

As much as I have always loved it I have never loved it more than I do right now in October 2008. In September I went to Duke University Hospital to have spinal surgery to correct a common ailment called stenosis. I had not been in a hospital as a patient since 1961.

When I returned to Fayetteville the town closed around me like a band of angels. A new rug had been delivered to make my house warmer, the Orkin man had come to spray for spiders, John Tucker McCormick (starting quarterback for a Fayetteville junior high school football team) had mowed my yard and swept my porches and sidewalks for leaves and hickory nuts, the athletic club had put up the swimming pool bubble so I'd have a warm place to recuperate, and the university where I teach had allowed me to have a large black recliner moved into the classroom where I teach my classes. It looks hilarious in the room, like a scene from a Pinter play. All I need are some Fritos and a case of bottled water and maybe a television set.

People I barely knew left notes in my mailbox asking to help or drive me places, wishing me luck. My students had written brilliant stories and nonfiction pieces and printed worksheets for our workshops.

Not to mention the weather these past weeks has been perfect, cool and clear, seventies in the daytime and fifties at night. The trees turned gold and red and yellow and violet and there was a full moon to remind me of the one I followed thirty-two years ago to lead me to this refuge.

My Paris and My Rome, Part II

IT IS THE HOT, DARK HEART OF SUMMER IN THIS SMALL TOWN that I love. Fireworks have been going off sporadically for several nights, and the teenagers next door are playing water polo in the afternoons in the swimming pool their professor parents built for them this year.

Down the street a four-year-old girl is riding her tricycle madly around the circular driveway of her parents' home. It seems only yesterday that I walked by the house one morning and saw a pink ribbon on the mailbox. Now she is a tricycle racer, her long curly hair hanging rakishly down over her eyes, her concentration and speed all you need to know about the power of our species.

Last week the painting contractor who painted the exterior of my house gave me a discount for my patience while he had a stent put in an artery leading to his heart. (The attending nurse in the surgery is my weekend workout partner. She also attended the emergency surgery that saved the life of the game and fish genius who traps squirrels for me when they eat the trim on my house.) During the prolonged painting job, I took to spending the part of the afternoons when I would normally be taking a nap down at a nearby coffee shop reading newspapers and drinking herbal tea. I ran into the president of a local bank who has recently retired to devote himself to building a natural science museum and planetarium in Fayetteville. We already have plenty of dinosaurs. Some farseeing biologists at the University of Arkansas collected them years ago. They have been saved in a small, musty museum on the campus that was recently closed, to the ire of many of the professors. (There is always plenty of ire in a college town, accompanied by a plethora of long-winded letters to the editors of the local newspapers and magazines. Nuclear power, pollution, cruelty to animals, war and cutting down trees are contenders for space, but the closing or shutting down of anything at the university is a top contender.)

Fayetteville now has sixty-two thousand people, but it still seems like the much smaller place I found when I was forty years old and adopted as my home. I had driven up into the northwest Arkansas hills to spend a semester in the writing program at the University of Arkansas, where I now teach. The moment I left the flatlands and began to climb into the Ozark Mountains, I fell in love with the place. There is a welcoming naturalness to the land, and it is reflected in the people. I immediately felt at home in Fayetteville and I still feel that way. Even when I didn't know everyone in town, I felt like I knew them. I lived in small towns in southern Indiana and southern Illinois when I was young, and Fayetteville has always reminded me of those places. There are many people here from the Deep South, but the heart of the place belongs to the Midwest. It is hill country, surrounded by farmland. There are never aristocracies in such places. There aren't enough people to be divided into groups. In the schools of small midwestern towns, the only aristocracies are of beauty, intelligence, and athletic prowess. I had been living in New Orleans, in a world of privilege, and I was never comfortable there. I have lived most of my life in small towns, and I'm in the habit of knowing and talking to everyone.

But I think it is the beauty of the hill country that really speaks to my heart. My ancestors are highland Scots, and my father's home in north Alabama is so much like northwest Arkansas I have the same allergies in both places. Besides, I like to watch water run downhill. After years in the flatlands, I am still delighted at the sight of rain running down my hilly street after a storm. I also like to watch it run down steep steps, before you even get to the thrill of camping north of here and watching it run over real waterfalls near the Buffalo River.

Most of all, this is where I write. Ever since the first night I spent in this town, I have been inspired to write by being here. When people in my family ask me why I live so far away from all of them, I always answer, because it's where I write. The place closes around me and makes me safe and makes me want to sing.

After thirty years of living here, I think I know everyone in town. I cannot walk down a street without seeing people I know or passing places where things occurred that mattered to me. Some of the people I loved have died, but it seems they have never left the place. Their children and grandchildren are here and their legacies: in buildings and businesses or in the town's collective memory. Some are remembered in statues and plaques, and some for things they said or wrote, and others for the places where they walked and lived. People love each other here. It's a habit and a solace in times of trouble.

I live in a glass-and-stone-and-redwood house built by an architect who won the Gold Medal of the American Institute of Architects. I bought the house for a pittance several years before he won the award, and I spend my spare time keeping it in working order. It is on two acres of land. I have deer on the lot behind the house and enough squirrels and turtles and rabbits and foxes and coons and possums to supply several petting zoos. Not to mention crows and redbirds and mockingbirds and woodpeckers and bluebirds and robins and an occasional itinerant roadrunner.

The first novel I wrote was set in Fayetteville, using many of the real people and places as background for the adventures of a poorly disguised autobiographical heroine named Amanda McCamey. (I disguised her by making her thinner, kinder, and braver than I was at the time.) The novel was really about Fayetteville. Here is how I described it in the novel.

Fayetteville, Arkansas. Fateville, as the poets call it. Home of the Razorbacks. During certain seasons of the year the whole town seems to be festooned with demonic red hogs charging across bumper stickers, billboards, T-shirts, tie-clasps, bank envelopes, quilts, spiral notebooks, sweaters. Hogs. Hog country. Not a likely place for poets to gather, but more of them keep coming every year. Most of them never bother to leave. Even the ones that leave come back all the time to visit.

Fateville, Home of the Hogs. Also, poets, potters, painters, musicians, woodcarvers, college professors, unwashed doctors, makers of musical instruments.

Fayetteville, Arkansas. Beautiful little wooded mountain town. Lots of poets. No money. Clear air, clean rivers, wonderful skies. Nothing to do all day but go to school and make things and wait for the mail.

Fayetteville, sitting on its hills and valleys in the extreme northwest corner of the state of Arkansas. The Ozarks, high ground. Where weather from four directions meets . . . Hard to scrape a living from these hills. Hard to leave once you learn to love its skies and seasons. Seasons appearing right on time like seasons in a children's book. Fall, a riot of red and yellow maples, winter, with enough snow for sleds, spring, coming over the hills like a field of dancers, bringing jonquils, dandelions, violets, pussywillow, celandine, sedge, and trout lily, turning the creeks into rivers.

Stars, clouds, storms, rain, snow eagles. Wild weather and people who work for a living and women who wash their own underwear.

Amanda has fallen in love with a world where the postman makes stained glass windows, the Orkin man makes dueling swords, the bartender writes murder mysteries, the waitress at the Smokehouse reads Nietzsche on her lunch break.

"Where in the name of God are you going?" Everyone in New Orleans kept asking Amanda.

"To Fayetteville, Arkansas," she replied. "My Paris and my Rome."

OCTOBER 19, 2008

Living with Light

❧⟊❧

I AM A LIGHT HEARTED PERSON WHO LOVES EARLY MORNING AND late afternoon. I love having the moon peek in a window where I have never noticed it shining before. I love the beauty of sunrise and sunset, the reds and golds and mauves as light enters and leaves the world.

So I keep on living year after year in the wonderful, light-filled, Japanese-influenced house that Fay Jones built when he was a young architect. It has concrete floors and is freezing cold in the winter. The entrances are so short that my tall grandchildren have to bend over to get in the front door. It requires constant attention and is expensive to maintain.

But it is my home and I cannot imagine living in any other house. There are windows everywhere, long banks of windows and skylights and a stone and concrete entrance with a pond that is covered by slanting windows that were set in stone with lead. If one of them breaks, the company that puts them in comes out and men stand around with their hands on their hips telling younger men how impossible it is going to be to replace the huge broken panes and how long it is going to take to do the job. I make them coffee and cheer them up and tell them it has been done before and can be done again.

I hope someday a wealthy person will own this house and make the repairs it still requires and have the redwood sealed and refinished so the house will look as Fay meant for it to look. For now I take care of it as well as I can and love its workmanship and design as much as anyone can love the place where they live.

~ ~ ~

Before I owned one of his houses I met Fay Jones at a small dinner party at Roy Reed's house. Fay and I formed an instant simpatico. I am a working artist, a successful, published writer. At the time I met Fay I was at the top of my form and had just won the National Book Award. Fay and I talked long and hard about our work and the joys of work and the problems of work. We were two charismatic people giving each other everything we had to give, understanding, respect, offering friendship.

We were in the dining room of the house Fay had just built for Roy and Norma Reed. It is far out in the country on a gravel road and was designed to look like a barn, a whimsical idea of Roy's perhaps. I liked the house but I didn't understand how anyone could live there. I later learned that the only way to understand one of Fay's houses is to live in it. It won't give up its secrets on a few visits. You have to live in it season after season and year after year to appreciate and understand the workmanship and genius. The genius for me is the way light makes its way around my house as the days and seasons go by, visions in rain and panoramas in snow and ice.

I have known several young architects as they began their careers and built their first houses. One of them was a true genius and was my close friend until his death. I know the problems architects have trying to stay true to their visions while pleasing their customers. Someone has to pay for all that concrete and mortar and lumber and stone and brick and roofing. Writers have problems also but we can make mistakes without costing thousands of dollars. Meeting Fay Jones meant a lot to me and I cherish that first meeting and the knowledge that we really liked each other.

A year after that first meeting I flew to Fayetteville on a spring day to buy a new house. I had been living in Jackson, Mississippi, near my family for a year and had sold my small Fayetteville house on Mt. Sequoyah. I wanted something larger so my growing number of grandchildren could come and visit.

A realtor named Merlee Harrison met my plane and took me to her house to spend the night. Early the next morning we had breakfast and set out to look for houses. We went into three or four uninspiring places and were beginning to despair. "Is there a Fay Jones house on the market?" I asked. "I know I can't afford one but let's look."

"There is one," she answered. "But it's in terrible shape. I'd hate to even show it to you."

"Show me. I want to see it."

"Well, it's on Mt. Sequoyah," she said. "But not on the side you used to live on."

All the way to the house she told me the reasons I shouldn't buy it. It had been on the market for a long time. It was in terrible condition. The last owners had let three German shepherds live inside. They had carpeted the scored, concrete floors. The wood was in bad condition. I wasn't going to like it. It would be too much for me to take care of.

We drove up in the driveway. A brilliant yellow forsythia bush lit up the path of the fallen fence. There was no garage or carport. One of the past owners had closed in the garage to make a guest room.

The huge yard was full of blooming spring bushes but it was overgrown and uncared for. The exterior of the house was unfinished redwood that was turning gray and black from mold. The screen doors were broken and half off their hinges.

"I told you," Merlee said.

We went inside and I began to walk around the space. Windows everywhere, light everywhere, even though it was now falling on dust and spider webs and the really terrible stained carpet.

"How much do they want for it?" I asked.

"A hundred and forty," she said. "They've come down twice."

"Offer them a hundred and ten," I said. "I can fix this place."

Merlee kept shaking her head. "I can fix it," I insisted. "I like all the windows. I like the room made out of the garage. I like the stone.

I like the lot. I can fix it. I know I can. Make them an offer. Tell them it's final. I don't want to bargain."

The owners accepted my offer. They had given up on the house and were building a new one out in the country.

"One proviso," I told Merlee, who went to the closing for me. "They have to pull out all those carpets and take down every single thing that is nailed to any wall anywhere on the inside or outside of the house. Every flower pot, every barometer, flagpole holder, everything of any kind. I want a clean slate."

A few months later I moved into the house. I lived in one bedroom until my furniture arrived from Jackson. Fay and Maurice Jennings had come out and inspected the damage and sent me a team of men to work on the interior wood. Tom January sent another team to work on the floors. Merlee found housekeepers to clean the windows and the walls. Day by day, week by week, it began to look like a house Fay Jones had designed and built. Most of all it began to be my house. I began to know it, to understand the amazing care with which it had been built. Fay visited me several times during the cleanup. "Italian stonemasons laid those stones," he told me. "They used to sing work songs while they worked."

To this day I can hear their songs when I walk onto the back patio and look at the amazing stone wall that supports the somewhat cracked but still strong and deep foundation.

I have owned the house since 1987. About ten years ago I began to have to paint parts of the house. I suffer from terrible mold allergies and the accumulated mold in the untreated redwood was making me so sick that my allergist, who had visited the house, said, "You have to move or die. This house is an allergist's nightmare."

The pond in the entranceway is walled with beautiful native stone. Ferns grow out of the stone. The pond was designed to catch ground water as that side of the house is dug into the north side of a hill. When it rained the stone wall was a waterfall. I kept the pond full of water treated with small amounts of chlorine and filled with tropical fish. The small ecosystem worked perfectly until my allergies became so terrible I couldn't breathe and had to take asthma medicine.

I refused to sell the house and leave. The house is my home and I love it. So I sealed up the pond and got rid of the fish. I called a painting contractor and painted the mold-infested walls with mold-resistant paint. Later I was forced to paint the entire house. I could not afford to have all that wood treated by experts, so I did what I had to do to continue to live in the house.

I like the painted walls. I love the design and space of the house but I don't like to live in dark brown rooms. I am unrepentant about painting the wood, although Fay Jones purists are mad at me for doing it. Fay built houses for people to live in. He loved my living in one of his houses and told me he didn't mind my painting it if that was what I had to do.

Fay designed the house in 1957–59. It was finished in 1960. He built it for a G. E. engineer named N. F. Harmon who planned on living in it with his new wife. Unfortunately Mr. Harmon died soon after the house was completed and his wife was too sad to live in it alone so the house never had the owner for whom it was built. I think that explains things like much of the wood being unfinished.

The house has had six owners. I'm sure they all loved it as much as I love it and, like me, couldn't afford to take care of it perfectly. I am charmed by the evidence of things previous owners did to solve the problems of living in a house built by a genius. The huge beautiful stone fireplace doesn't draw well unless it has a very big fire going. Someone covered the entrance to the fireplace with an expensive glass cover. I bless them for having done that. When I bought the house there were thermometers everywhere, inside and out. After a few freezing winters, a flood from pipes breaking in the attic during an ice storm, and huge bills from the electric company I can understand the thermometers. I am on constant watch for winter problems. I leave the television on the weather channel, let faucets drip and have a plumbing company drain the house of water if I'm gone for any time. I moved the electric water heater out of the attic, had the heating system replaced and moved the collapsed ducts out of their concrete housing. Unfortunately the ducts had to be put in the ceilings where they are not as useful as they were on the floors. As I said I have done what I could afford to do in my wonderful house but it is not always what would have been the best idea.

When Fay and the G. E. engineer planned the house electricity was dirt cheap so the entire house is powered by electricity, including the dozens of light bulbs which were in the (at the time) very novel recessed lighting. Previous owners had run extension cords all over the house and through the walls in an attempt to add lighting with lamps that used less electricity and gave more light. After I bought the house I brought in an electrician who is also a Springdale fireman and he went crazy pulling extension cords out of walls and telling me how lucky I was that I wasn't dead. I had waited until I got shocked trying to plug in a lamp before I called the electrician.

I have learned many things while restoring this house. Also, I understand Zen concepts. This house is pure Zen. For the first ten years I lived here I couldn't get the roof to stop leaking. I had two inexpensive roofs put on the house and it still leaked. Finally, one spring I hired a man who seemed to understand the roof. He came out one morning with a truckload of Mexican workers, none of whom spoke English except the driver, who was crippled. When the workers hit a snag they would go get the driver. They would carry him to the worksite and confer with him. He would tell me what was happening. Then they would carry him back to the truck where he read and listened to the radio. The three days I spent with the Mexican workers were pure Zen. One of them was taking an English-as-a-second-language course from a friend of mine. Between his studies and my broken Spanish we had very nice conversations. I gave him advice about how to deal with his teenage daughter and he assured me that this time my roof would not leak. He was almost correct. The first time it rained there was a small flood in my office but the roofers came back

out that afternoon and fixed it and it has never leaked again. In heavy
rains I still walk around the house checking the places where it used
to leak but so far the Mexican magic is holding.

I have copies of the original blueprints of the house. I remember being in Fay's office one morning and having Maurice Jennings walk in
the door and hand me the blueprints. I had not asked for them. They
were a surprise.

I love having the blueprints. I marvel at the details, knowing this
wonderful house was once a vision Fay developed while standing
on an undeveloped hill on Mt. Sequoyah. He sited the house on the
north side of the hill, dug in to protect it from tornadoes, which come
from the south in this area. I feel completely safe here in any weather. I had a wooden cover made for the only window in a room that
was intended to be a garden room but has had many uses. When my
son lived here it was a darkroom, now it houses the hot water heater
that was once in the attic. It is also used to store the rugs I put on
the floors in the winter. In summer I like the floors bare so I can see
the precise way they were scored to guide the builders and carpenters, most of whom had never built a house with so many cabinets
and so few walls. Fay taught a group of local carpenters how to build
his houses. He told me he was on the site almost every day when
my house was being built. Mr. Harmon was also there, directing the
complicated electrical circuits for one of the first all-electric houses
in the area.

There are many places in the house where I could take shelter
from a tornado but the garden room is my first choice. If there are
tornado warnings I put pillows and blankets on top of the stored
rugs, add a battery operated radio and some crackers and bottled
water and my cellular phone. I won't need books as the cabinets in
the room are already filled with books. Fay's cabinets make excellent
bookshelves.

Maurice and Fay were always so generous and kind to me about the
house. I kept waiting for a bill but one never came. They even drew

blueprints for screen doors to replace the ones that were broken. I had the doors made by a local woodworker and they are so lovely several friends have asked permission to copy them for their homes.

The house is beautiful and peaceful and Zen and the site on which it was built is perfect for the house. No matter how many floods or ice storms assault the house it dries out and stands strong. Someone told me the reason it is built of California redwood is that a local builder imported a warehouse full of redwood and when he went broke Fay bought it from him for a song. I was glad to hear that story whether or not it is true. I had always wondered why a young architect would import redwood when we live in a hardwood forest.

Every day I thank Fay (and the G. E. engineer) for the gift of this exciting, interesting home. Light is everywhere. The sun shines in the windows, it peeks in unexpectedly from a skylight over the fireplace, triangulates down across the stone entryway, delights me in any season. The moon shines in the glass windows over the pond, ferns sprout from nowhere in the stone wall. Everything is quiet and everything is a surprise.

There are so many stories to tell. The house was built to fit in between two hickory trees. The trees are huge now and produce many hickory nuts in August and September. The local squirrels adore the nuts. They swarm here to make huge messes of nut shells on the back patio and the front entranceway. One year they stashed hundreds of nuts in the overhangs over the patio. It took two workmen days to uncover all the hiding places and remove the nuts and repair the wood.

Later that fall the angry squirrels began to chew the redwood trim off the house, both on the front and back of the house. I have since talked to many owners of wooden houses who have had the same problem in Fayetteville.

I called the game and fish commission and they sent a retired game and fish expert out to my house to trap the squirrels. It cost twenty dollars a squirrel to have them removed and relocated over a period of three years. Much trim was destroyed during that time but I got to become friends with Mr. Cecil Gibbs, a brilliant man who knows everything about the large and small animals of the Ozarks. He traps animals for the Walton family in Bentonville and holds records in the delta for the largest beavers trapped near rice fields. Several years ago he had a heart attack while hunting on a cold November day. He managed to drive himself to the hospital where his life was saved by a beautiful young woman who is one of my exercise buddies at the local health club. I consider this more proof of the totally Zen magic of my Fay Jones house.

It occurs to me, especially in cold weather, that I should sell the house and get a small apartment. Several times I have even gone so far as to call a realtor, but I can't go through with it. I love this house. We have been through a lot together. The house is all on one floor. If I ever had to be in a wheelchair I could live here with no trouble. I'd just move through the house on wheels, waiting to see what was going to happen.

Last year I made it impossible to sell the house by building a covered lap pool in the backyard. The pool is to help me recover from back surgery so I can put off being in the wheelchair for many more years. I can't leave now. I'm here to stay. I'm dug in. This is my home.

SEPTEMBER 3, 2009

My Paris and My Rome, Part III

SINCE I WROTE THAT LAST ESSAY I HAVE DONE AN EXCITING AND unexpected thing. I sold the large Fay Jones house that none of my family ever came to visit any more because they have too many children to drive six hundred miles to see me when they can wait until I'm in Ocean Springs and come to the beach.

I made up my mind to sell it, called the toughest, best realtor in town, painted and fixed anything that was broken and sold it in a week for the price I asked for it.

My dream came true. I sold it to a doctor and his wife who have the money and time to rebuild it to suit the contemporary world. The doctor had lived in Fayetteville while he did his residency in general medicine, then moved to Alaska for seventeen years. When he and his wife were here they had lived near Mt. Sequoyah and dreamed of owning a Fay Jones house. They flew here for two days to search for a house; he was moving here to teach medicine in our new medical school. They walked in my house one morning and bought it that afternoon.

Then I went out with the realtor and found a wonderful brick condominium in a new neighborhood with children and teenagers and people walking their dogs in the morning and all sorts of things I like because I'm a small-town girl and don't need to live on two acres of land in a house that has to be worshipped and served.

I had heard about downsizing and now I have done it. My new place is clean and new and pretty and has a garage with a door that opens at the touch of a button and a huge attic where I can store my papers and first editions of my books (for my grandchildren).

I loved my old neighborhood and my neighbors and will always love them but my new neighborhood is young and full of life and four minutes from the Fayetteville Athletic Club and three minutes from the mall and four minutes from the hospital and all my doctors' offices. One of my old neighbors said, "You have moved to your mothership."

The best thing was giving away recliners and refrigerators and beds to young people who needed them and came and carried them away.

The most difficult thing was trying to find a way to send a Chickering baby grand piano to Mobile, Alabama, to one of my great-grandchildren who has recently started taking piano lessons. I had almost decided to go on and crowd it into the small kitchen of my new condo but it would have cost as much money to move it across town as it would to get it to Mobile.

A wealthy friend saved me. For a gift she sent her family's movers to pick it up and take it to the little boy I call MK2. She was tired of hearing me worry about it.

There was a wonderful scene the morning after I moved out of the Fay Jones house. The people who bought the house had asked me to keep on living in the house for five weeks to take care of it until they arrived on August 15, 2013. I moved out, in a terrible rainstorm, on August 14. (Managing somehow to throw away or lose a large doubled grocery bag which contained all my checkbooks to four bank accounts and my Merrill Lynch account which made the first week of my new life a hurried and interesting time closing all the bank accounts and opening new ones and learning that a branch of my bank was one mile from my new place with a great coffee bar, wonderful vice presidents and more new friends. Also, I memorized the new bank account numbers to prove that I don't have to go to an old folks home yet.)

Rain or no rain a company called Two Men and a Truck, two Mexican women and I managed to move everything except the piano from the Fay Jones house into the newly painted and floored condo and by six o'clock I was unpacking boxes. It was not until late the next morning that I realized the grocery sack with my financial life was absolutely, positively lost or thrown away. No checks on the cancelled accounts were ever presented to any of the banks so I think the checkbooks are out in the Tontitown landfill underneath whatever else the good people of Fayetteville threw away that Thursday.

Early on the morning of August 15 I took three cleaning ladies over to the Fay Jones house to clean it up for the new owners and to meet the movers who were coming to take apart and send the Chickering baby grand to Mobile.

We got there about seven-thirty in the morning and while the movers were disassembling my precious old piano I wandered around the house deciding where the cleaning ladies should begin.

In my bedroom, where I had spent most of my nights for twenty-six years, I found the handsome doctor and his adorable wife sound asleep on the floor in sleeping bags. Their movers from Alaska had called them the day before, while they were driving two cars across the United States, stopping to see old friends and relatives and their children, having a leisurely drive to their new home and work, and told them they had to hurry to Fayetteville as their furniture would be there by noon on the fifteenth.

The doctor and his wife had driven like mad and gotten to the house about four in the morning. What wonderful, brave, adventurous new owners the house has now.

The first day that it snowed in Fayetteville their first winter there, last winter, they packed all their ski gear into the back of a truck, parked it going downhill Eastwood Drive, as I had told them they must do when there is a forecast for snow, woke the next morning and went out and drove down the snow covered hill to a nearby hilly park and skied most of the day. Delightful, adventurous Alaskans are among us, my house has new owners worthy of its storied past, and I have new friends who call me up and read me the mail that still occasionally comes to their mailbox. Every month or so I drive over to the house to pick up the mail and watch the amazing building projects going on around it. A brilliantly designed three-car garage with open sides and heating, a new deck with a beautiful drainage system, and a cover for the swimming pool which has lowered the gas bill by eighty percent. I wish I had thought of that.

This is not the end of this story I'm sure but it's most of what has happened so far.

Plus, I adore my downsized life and wish I'd done that sooner than I did.

February 2007,
Homage to William Shawn

───────❦───────

I AM TEACHING A READINGS COURSE IN CREATIVE NONFICTION but it should be called a course in the editing genius of William Shawn (who was the editor of *The New Yorker* for many years).

Slouching Towards Bethlehem by Joan Didion, *In Cold Blood* by Truman Capote, *The Curve of Binding Energy* by John McPhee are a few examples of the perfect prose that came from his editing. Every book he edited that I teach holds up. Most of them were written in the nineteen seventies but I can find nothing written now that page after page comes up to the brilliance and perfection Shawn was able to demand and call up in his writers. After I teach the books to my graduate students they teach them to the undergraduates. Soon I will have to make up a new course as the undergraduate English majors will already have read the books I assign when they become our graduate students, as many of them do.

A wonderful thing is happening in the English Department of the University of Arkansas. Talented students who have been brought into the college with our best scholarships are flocking to take writing classes in our English Department and many of them are so good we are letting them take seminars in our Master of Fine Arts Program in Creative Writing.

At the same time, post–nine/eleven, we have a hiring freeze and a freeze on raises and five of our best professors have died or retired. The three who retired taught long past the time when they should have retired but stayed bravely on to help out after the crisis.

Now we are in a situation where we have an extra-large number of students and fewer professors to teach the core subjects. Also, we have lost two professors in the Creative Writing Program and have not been allowed to replace them. We are letting extra people into all our classes, which is not good in the writing workshops. Somehow, everyone seems to want to live up to the challenge, however, and the feeling around Kimpel Hall is good. We will, by God, teach them what we know. At least that's how I feel. It's a good semester.

I'm proud to be here. I still don't like to go to department parties because I don't drink and don't like to talk to people when they are drinking but this week I will even go to a party I have decided. I intend to be the first one there and the first to leave, however. At least I won't have to watch the students drinking in the presence of the professors. I think that is wrong and won't participate in it.

By the end of the William Shawn–influenced nonfiction class one student had a long, brilliant manuscript which won our coveted Walton Fellowship for his senior year here. He has not sent it to agents or publishers yet but will soon I hope. He keeps thinking he will find a better ending but this is nonfiction and sometimes life doesn't give us a lot of choices in our endings.

Neither is the mother of his child going to quit drinking and come back to him and his child. We can't save everyone we love. Even writing a brilliant, loving, tender, dazzlingly comprehending book about what caused the problem cannot save her. But it might save him and it might be helpful to the child someday. Every day I say my crazy first and second and third star wishes for the real people and for the lovely gentle book.

The Courts of Love

An Anniversary

DECEMBER 29, 2009

FORTY-EIGHT YEARS AGO TODAY I MARRIED JUDGE JAMES NELSON Bloodworth of Decatur, Alabama, in the Presbyterian Church of Courtland, Alabama, underneath the forty-thousand-dollar stained glass window my father had given the church the year before.

I was wearing a blue silk suit which my aunt Louise Hitch Gilchrist had ironed for me that morning in my grandmother's guest room. I was drinking champagne and so was she and so were my best friends, Allison and Anne Bailey. We were giddy by the time we left for the church in my father's Cadillac.

I had spent the night before the wedding alone with my grandmother. I was sleeping in the iron double bed where she used to pretend to be the little people inside the radio telling their stories. "Let me out," she would scream. "Get me out of here."

It should have been a metaphor for the wedding that was about to take place. To make up for my drinking too much I was marrying the most respectable man in town. Except when I was drinking, I was respectable. Since I quit drinking forty years ago I have become almost entirely respectable and contemptuous of people who are not.

I don't like excess. I'm a Scot. I hate waste. I like order. I like the world in which I grew up except for the problems caused by whiskey.

Before I went to bed the night before my wedding to the judge I went into my grandmother's small orderly bedroom and knelt beside her bed and let her bless me and wish me a happy and useful life. "He is a good man," she said. "Be kind to him."

"I will," I promised. "I'll try as hard as I can." I wanted to be a good wife and have an honorable life beside this fine man. He was forty-seven years old. I was twenty-four. He had been a major in the United States Army Judicial Corps. He had served all during the war and was in the army of occupation in the American sector of Germany for three years after the war.

He had been Phi Beta Kappa and Law Review at the University of Alabama School of Law. Later he would sit on the Alabama Supreme Court.

At the time of our marriage he was serving his second elected term as circuit judge of Madison County, Alabama.

I was a beautiful, rich, spoiled girl with two beautiful, small sons. They had hair the color of sunrise and wild black eyes and were powerful and strong and big for their ages. They were fearless and always in motion. I adored them as long as I didn't have to take care of them by myself. I had left my husband and come home to live with my family because they had maids and babysitters and my parents adored my little boys because they were the only grandsons. There were a lot of granddaughters but my father and brothers didn't want granddaughters. They wanted a dynasty and that required male children. They let me have or do anything I wanted as long as I kept having sons.

I loved my little boys. They were exactly what I had wanted except I didn't want them when I was twenty years old and twenty-one. I wanted to be a writer. I wanted the big world. I wanted to finish college and go to New York City and work at a publishing company and publish poems and magazine articles. I didn't want to spend my life taking care of small children.

In Praise of the Young Man

WHERE IS HE NOW, FOR WHOM I CARRY IN MY HEART
THIS LOVE, THIS PRAISE?
—Edna St. Vincent Millay

HE WAS TWENTY-SIX AND I WAS FORTY-FOUR. HE TOOK ME DOWN rivers in canoes and built fires in the woods for me and taught me not to be afraid. I followed him places I had always dreamed of going. When I was a child my father and my brothers would strike out for the woods, leaving me behind. This time I was not left behind. I was the cause of the expeditions. I was the girl sitting on the floor of the canoe reading fashion magazines while my beautiful lover guided the canoe over treacherous waters. Could I have resisted such seduction? Could anyone have resisted it?

I lost ten pounds the first month I knew him. I lost twenty years. At a time when most women my age are worrying about menopause, I thought I was *pregnant* when I stopped menstruating. That was completely impossible since I had had a tubal ligation years before; still, the idea was exciting, and later I wrote a novel out of the fantasy and made a lot of money from it.

He taught me to shoot pool. He bought me a baseball shirt with blue sleeves. He made love to me one afternoon in the backseat of a car. I had never made love in an automobile. I thought it was hilarious. I thought it was the freest and funniest thing I had ever done.

Beside a lake, in a remote part of a national park, I took off my underpants and made love in the backseat of a car.

He taught me to sing. He taught me that if you know the words
you won't forget the tune. He taught me to sing "Mommas, Don't Let
Your Babies Grow Up to Be Cowboys." He would let me sing it over
and over again when we went on car trips.

He sang to me. He would take his guitar out of his guitar case and
sit on my piano bench tuning it and playing chords for a long time
before he began to sing. He would sing songs he was composing and
songs he was practicing and finally, because he knew I was waiting
for it, he would sing, "Dance with me, I want to be your partner."

It was the first song he had ever sung to me. On the day we met
he played it for me on a balcony at sundown. An hour later, when
the world was dark, he asked me to marry him. This is the way to
win a woman. This is the way a woman wants to fall in love. And
he did dance with me. He danced with me in my living room and in
nightclubs and on sidewalks at dark in distant cities. He danced with
me as if I were an extension of his own body, and his joy in dancing
made me graceful.

When I met him I had just moved to a small town in the Ozark
Mountains. One reason I had moved there was to be near the woods.
I longed for woods, for rivers and wilderness. After I met the young
man, he became my guide.

He would drop anything to go camping. It would pour down rain
for several days and he would turn to me and say, "This rain is going
to fill up all the rivers. We should go down one while we can. When
they're full the sissies won't be in the way." Then we would throw
a change of clothes into a plastic bag, grab the tent, and be out the
door. One morning we set off down the Buffalo River when the water was two feet above the bridges. I don't know how we talked the
canoe shop into renting us a canoe, except the owner knew the young
man and trusted him not to get us killed.

He could guide a canoe down the river without seeming to move
a muscle. His old Cherokee grandfather had taught him to fish and

hunt and live in the woods. He didn't like equipment. A cigarette lighter and a sack of crackers and cheese was all he needed to enter the woods and live for days.

What did we talk about during those long days and nights when we were alone on rivers and riverbanks and in woods? I think we talked about ourselves, telling the stories of our lives, laughing about what people were saying about us behind our backs. We thought it was hilarious that people thought I was old and he was young. We were not old or young to each other. We were in love and had been since the day we met.

Perhaps we only imagined that people were talking about us *behind our backs.* The people who were interested in us were over at my house talking *to us* and listening to us talk about ourselves. A passionate love affair is a strange attractor. People cannot stay away from happiness and joy.

A famous scientist in town became the mentor of our love affair. He was seventy years old and had degrees from Oxford and Edinburgh. He loved to be around the young man and me. He would sit in my living room and watch us interact and later he would talk to me about it. Once, when I said I thought I should end the relationship and force the young man to find a woman his own age, the scientist said to me, "Why are women always thinking they can tell men what to want? All men don't have to want the same things. Men are as complicated as women are, although women don't want to believe that's true. Why do you keep questioning and probing the happiness you have? Why can't you just be content with it?"

"They aren't all as complicated as women," I replied.

"The good ones are," he answered. "The only ones you would be interested in knowing. The ones who write songs about you."

The young man had been writing a song about me. He had taken the central premise of a book I had written and turned it into a beautiful, small lyric. The song was plaintive, simple, clean. It said the thing he never said to me. *I love you and I will lose you because this is a land of dreams.*

~ ~ ~

What were people saying about us? Young artists around town were basically tolerant. The older male writers wanted to think it was a joke and talk me out of it. The women mostly understood or else they thought it was good revenge on older men who go out with younger women. I thought all of their reactions were interesting insights into their own needs and personalities. To tell the truth I didn't give a damn what any of them thought.

A journalist in the town where I live says I used to wear the young man like a bangle on a bracelet. I did occasionally like to take him around people my own age and watch him charm them. He was a charming man, intelligent and well read, with a deep feeling of good-will toward other people.

There are deeper truths to what went on between us. On the day I met the young man I had just learned that my daughter-in-law was carrying my first grandchild. I was in ecstasy at this news. Perhaps I fell in love with the young man to be part of all that fecundity and life. I had these two great happinesses at the same time.

I would wake from sleep during those months in a state of bliss. Every shaft of light seemed intense and beautiful. The taste and feel of water was almost unbearable in its beauty, clarity, purity. Every tree and flower and change of weather seemed charged with meaning and with purpose.

There were darker truths to the relationship. There were things about his life I could never understand or accept. There were dark, controlling parts of my personality that surprised and wounded him. I was full of old selfishness, anxieties, and fears. He was full of old resentments. When we would try to live together, these elements would ignite and burn.

This was not a small fling. It lasted on and off for many years.

My oldest son was enraged by the affair. He thought I should be content to be a grandmother. By the time he met the young man, my grandchild had been born, and my son thought I should follow in my mother's footsteps and devote my life to my progeny.

The young man's family was probably equally unhappy about the love affair, but I never knew the details of that. As much as we could we stayed away from our families. We tried to protect each other from their intrusions, and I think we did a good job of that. Once, after we had known each other for many years, I took the young man to Mississippi to meet my parents. They called me up two nights later. They were eighty-two at the time. I was fifty-seven. "That won't do," my father said when he got me on the phone. "This business with the young man has got to stop."

My mother got on the phone. "You will have to get rid of him," she added. "I'm sure your children are embarrassed to death by this."

"Nothing I could do to them would be as bad as the things they have done to me," I answered in the nasty tone I reserve for talking to my mother. "I am fifty-seven years old, Mother. I am hanging up."

The young man and I were always hanging up on the world. Nothing the outside world did seemed to be able to harm what went on between us. We made each other happy and we made each other laugh and we made each other strong. When we were together love was its own protection, a barrier against reality.

Of course it had to end. I told him in the beginning I would be his girl until I was fifty years old. I was almost sixty when it finally really ended. We had broken up and made up many times during those years but always without rancor or ill will. The truth was we couldn't stay away from each other. We had created a paradise when we first met, and when we were apart we would long to have it back. He would call me or I would call him and within an hour we would be in bed. We would lie in each other's arms and tell the story of when we met and fell in love and told the world to go to hell. We shared a fabulous story of who we had been together, of what we had dared and what we had created.

I have been in psychotherapy for many years. I know that the young man was a surrogate for my sons who had grown up and gone off to have lives of their own. I know that for him I was the mother all men dream of having. The mother who is their sole possession. The mother who adores them without question. I know that these psychological realities were the grounds for our disagreements and the reason the relationship could never last. I knew this while it was going on but it did not change a thing.

Love is a goddess. It is the honey to end all honeys. No one turns down Aphrodite when she comes to call. The old Greeks knew how to create a metaphor. The goddess of love with her satisfied, enigmatic smile. Her little son beside her with his quiver of arrows. He lifts his bow, he takes aim, he shoots, and a man or woman falls into a spell from which there is no escape.

Perhaps I loved him because he was different from the other men I had known. He never turned on a television set. He was a small-town boy and read the local newspaper and liked knowing what was going on in the place where he lived. He didn't care what was happening in New York City or Washington, D. C. He wanted to know who was running for sheriff and what was on at the movies and who won the high school football games.

He taught me to love. Not just romantic love, and God knows it was romantic, but love of place. He would drive me around and show me places that he loved. He took me to see the place where his mother taught him how to swim. He was very sentimental about that small, weed-bordered lake. He always spoke of his mother with love and praise and because of that I knew I was safe to believe he loved me. A man who resents his mother will sooner or later resent you if he loves you.

None of that had much to do with young and old. Love is liking to be with another person. Having a good time in their presence, thinking you are good and valuable when you are with them.

I remember the first time he saw my forty-four-year-old body in a bathing suit. He was taking me swimming in a beautiful clear lake formed by the dammed-up waters of the White River. As usual he did not tell me where we were going. We took bathing suits and a lunch and got in the car and started driving. We drove for more than an hour, going north and west from home, going deep into the Ozark Mountains. We turned finally into a park and drove around and up to an overhang and parked the car and got out and started walking.

We walked down wide granite steps that had once been the top of a mountain. I learned to swim in a bayou in the Mississippi delta and I love the taste and feel of brown river water. We changed into our bathing suits in a grove of shrub trees. "This is the body of a forty-four-year-old woman in a bathing suit," I said. "What do you think?"

"I think you look wonderful," he said. "Hold my hand."

Then we walked down the granite steps to the water and he watched as I slid into the lake and started swimming. No man giving a woman diamonds ever had more pleasure or self-assurance in their gifts than he did in giving me that blessed lake.

Am I romanticizing all of this? Perhaps. I have had two great love affairs in my life. I don't think either of them need romanticizing.

I cherish the memory of that affair and I am always glad it happened. It made me understand my sons. It reminded me, at a time when many women are leaving such things behind, what passion is and does and causes, how it takes over and calls the shots and creates its own reality. As Edna St. Vincent Millay wrote, it is a "treasure never to be bartered by the hungry days."

Being Wooed

BEING WOOED IS WHEN A MAN SETS OUT TO AND MAKES YOU desire and love him, need him, dream of him, miss him when he's gone. A man could give me a Learjet, and I would certainly be glad, but that wouldn't necessarily make me want to hold him in my arms or marry him or bear his children. I have had three husbands and many lovers, but only one of them ever really wooed me. He was a young musician who gave me spontaneous, original gifts from his heart, desiring me while I was doing dishes, putting me in the car and taking me to see a waterfall without telling me where we were going, bringing me a baseball shirt on the first day of spring. The baseball shirt was white with blue sleeves, and when I put it on, he said, "Wear it with those velvet jeans. I go crazy when you wear those velvet jeans." An hour later I was out in the park watching him play softball with his old high-school basketball team. Life was beautiful and easy for this man, and when I was with him it seemed that way to me. He included me in everything he did. He offered me his whole world.

Other men I had been involved with had tried to figure out how to woo me, but there was nothing spontaneous about their efforts. I could always imagine the whole, dreary process as they remembered it was about to be my birthday or Christmas and marched duly out to search for something to give me—knowing all the while, and rightly, it probably wouldn't be anything I wanted, but at least I couldn't say they didn't try. It would be an expensive scarf with a horse-riding motif, a stiff arrangement of flowers sent by a secretary and usually delivered while I was out of town, or, occasionally, something with diamonds I would have to wear whether it suited me or not. I loved those men for their efforts, and I loved the way they waited to be praised, but still, something inside me always wanted to say: surprise me, serenade me, carve my name on a tree.

The way to woo a woman is to adore her. The thing women want is to be desired. When the musician made love to me, he said, I've never known such happiness, I think about you all day long, don't ever leave me, don't ever go away.

I think the other men I loved felt this way, but they couldn't bring themselves to admit it. Perhaps men are afraid of women, afraid of their need for us, dazzled by our delicacy and beauty. Perhaps they feel that if they tell us how much they love us, we will take advantage of them, and, of course, some of us will.

Being wooed is not the same thing as being seduced. When I was with the musician, I never felt I was being tricked or used. I felt something important was being made manifest. I never expected it to last forever, but I knew I was being changed by it. Even now, many years later, I remember that time without remorse or a sense of loss. I learned from that encounter, about love and its power to make the world seem wider and deeper, rich and timeless.

One reason the musician was able to woo me was that I allowed him to do it. I never let the powerful, successful men I fell in love with pursue me, because I was pursuing them so hot and heavy they could hardly get a gift in edgewise. The wooing I wanted from them was a wedding ring. When I was in love, the only thing that made me feel safe was complete commitment. I always asked men to marry me before they could ask me. My need was so terrible that I spoiled all possibility of surprise.

The musician managed to ask me first. He asked me the night I met him. It was spring, and new buds were on the trees, and the world seemed filled with poetry. The week after we met, he wrote a song about me and played it at a performance. What woman is immune to such wooing? We never did get married, but the fact that he had asked me made me secure.

A man who is not afraid to woo is a rare and lovely creature. My oldest granddaughter is being courted at the moment by an endearing young man. She came down the stairs on Valentine's Day dressed to go to dinner with him. He was waiting at the bottom of the stairs. When she was almost to the last stair, he opened a box and poured hundreds of rose petals at her feet. I think we are going to see a lot more of that young man.

There have been moments in my life when the most rigid or unlikely man would suddenly do something that seemed a dance of courtship. Once, a spoiled southern mama's boy dove from a yacht into a dangerous river in the dark to save me. Everything I thought I'd known about that man changed in an instant. I had insisted I could swim in any body of water and had jumped into the river to prove it, but the current was too strong, as he had told me it would be. When he saw I was in trouble, he saved me—and afterward he didn't say, "I told you so" or get mad at me for putting him in danger. I loved him on and off for several years afterward. Nothing he did in his spoiled, indulged life could make me forget what he had done when it mattered.

A writer I know told me she once fell in love with a man because he had a clothes dryer delivered to her house. She was young and poor and had to take her clothes to a laundromat to dry them. He saw a need and filled it.

The way to woo a woman is to give her what she needs before she knows she needs it, or to give her what she needs before she asks. A politician gave me the best present I have ever been given by a lover. It was a large book, hot off the presses, of photographs of earth taken from a satellite. He knew my interest in geology and gave me something I wanted that I didn't know existed.

I never know I need love until it is offered to me. Perhaps wooing is the way a man reminds a woman of the joy two people can give each other. Who cares if it's oedipal or electral or simple chemistry? It's still the honey to end all honeys. It's not for sale, this strange, rare happiness, but if it is, the coin of the realm is imagination.

Writing Maketh an Exact Man, Part II

I'VE BEEN THINKING ABOUT WRITING A SHORT PIECE ABOUT why I won't get a brain transplant. I have already decided not to undergo any more cancer screenings since no one in my huge extended family has ever had cancer and I'm not going to get it. I'm going to die of a stroke in my nineties like all my female ancestors, and sooner if I don't quit getting mad over the tackiness and fearmongering and wastefulness of the culture in which I live.

That being so, I am going to have to learn to love my own brain and its ways of hauling me around the world. I am often contemptuous, impatient, and condescending. I don't like people who have no self-discipline. I dislike drunks, dope addicts and obese people. I am also kind and generous and useful.

Until I began to tell people that I couldn't get a brain transplant I didn't know how to tell myself that it was all right to be myself. It's all right to tell people who drink too much and are fat that alcohol is highly concentrated sugar and they should stop drinking it, if they are really serious about losing weight. I used to feel guilty if I said that to someone who had asked my advice about losing weight. But it's the truth as I see it, and it is not possible for me to lie to people. I'm not good at it. If I know someone who has to be lied to then I don't want to see them anymore. It's a waste of my time and breath.

The reason to stop trying to change your nature is that it wastes time you could have spent using your native talents and skills to get some work done in the world. As Einstein said, to pay the world back for providing you with food and shelter and electricity and plumbing and love and entertainment.

I have pulled my punches as a writer off and on for thirty-seven years. The gloves are off. From now on I call it like I see it.

It is making me a much better writing teacher than I was when I began to try to learn to teach. Writing is hard work. It means thinking and rethinking each sentence, rethinking structure while trying to save the natural tone, trying to save the truth of what you write, to believe in the voice your brain gave you the sentence in. Most of what I know about writing in the last few years is couched in the language of singles tennis matches at the major tennis tournaments. I love sports metaphors. I was raised on them as a child and I have come back to them in my old age.

Play to win, don't limp to the finish, keep your eye on the ball, concentrate, focus, practice, practice, practice.

It is difficult to become a writer because the first thing you have to do is arrange a life that allows you to write. You have to be sober, hardworking, and in good health. You have to take care of your body and your brain. You can't let people waste your time. Take the telephone off the hook when you have work to do. Unplug the computer, except for the part you are using as a tool. I still use an electric typewriter so I can unplug everything in the house except for that and if the electricity goes off I can write very well on a legal pad with a number-two lead pencil.

I learned how to live as a writer by reading a book by Ernest Hemingway called *On Writing*. A young editor at Hemingway's publishers had gone through his writings and pulled out all the advice about how to be a writer. That editor is now the editor in chief of Little, Brown.

Meditations on Divorce

———————— ⌁ ————————

I HAVE PUT THIS ESSAY IN THE FORM OF MEDITATIONS BECAUSE I do not have a theory to expound. I do not want to "lead you to an overwhelming question." All I have to offer are the ideas I have been entertaining for many years as I watched myself, my friends, and my children live through painful and troubled times in the courts of love. The higher the intelligence, the slower the rate of maturation. This is true in phylogeny, ontogeny, and in our lives. The more intelligent and sensitive the person, the more likely they seem to have their relationships end in chaos. Perhaps the intelligence and sensitivity make it more difficult for them to endure relationships that have gone bad.

Here are some of the things I have observed.

Divorce is caused by stupid marriages. By people getting married when they are too young or because they are scared or because they think a wife or husband will "complete" them. And divorce is often a very good idea. It's certainly better than a loveless or ill-suited or painful marriage.

Children are the victims of divorce. Most grown men and women go on to other relationships and, except for wasting energy being angry at the person they have divorced or been divorced by, usually manage to learn a little something from the interchange. Of course, unless they are in some sort of therapy during the marriage or divorce, they generally go on to repeat the cycle, hopefully with someone at least slightly more suited to their real needs (which very few people ever acknowledge or examine, much less try to overcome or alter). Between them, my two brothers have married five women who look like my mother. Blond, blue-eyed, polite, quiet, gentle, inflexible. But neither of my brothers is interested in talking about animas or in seeing patterns in their behavior.

Not that years of psychoanalysis have made a dent in my program. Every man I have been involved with has been the oldest son of a powerful woman. In the deep and meaningful relationships, the ones that ended in marriage, they have usually been the oldest son of three brothers. My father is the oldest of three brothers and the son of a powerful mother.

Perhaps it does no good to know any of this. Perhaps it is impossible to choose who we love or want to breed with. Still, for me, the ability to articulate and understand my experience makes up somewhat for whatever inconvenience I have been caused by my unconscious strivings and yearnings.

"We can do what we want, but we can't want what we want," a wise man wrote, and this is, alas, the long and short and the *halter* of it.

Why do we make these crazy marriages that end in tragedy or divorce? Because we have mothers. When we are born we are held against the soft skin of our mothers. (Unless we are unlucky and lose our mothers, but that is another story.)

This sets us up to fall in love. The minute you take off your clothes and lie down beside the soft skin of another human being, the relationship is changed forever. This is the ground of being. This is the big, big story. I have often thought, now that I am in my late middle age, a time surely of reflection and surmise, that perhaps we were better off with arranged marriages. To allow our young men and women to go off and lie down beside anyone they find attractive is dangerous. It often leads to marriages where the partners are unequal in money, scope, intelligence, sophistication, culture. These inequities are of no importance to nature, who wants us to breed far away from our DNA (hybrid vigor, that mother and father of beauty, genius, stamina, brilliance), but they are fertile ground for disagreement when the initial attraction begins to wane.

I have known many wise and wonderful men and women who were good at everything but staying married. Well-meaning men and women, who entered marriages with the best and purest of intentions, have been shocked and stricken to find they could not maintain the love they felt for the person they married, or, worse, that they fell in love with "someone new," as the language so brilliantly puts it. A marriage is altered by such yearnings whether the adulterous heart acts on them or not.

Even the best among us are subject to Cupid and his arrows, to our unconscious wishes to re-create and recast our childhood, to fall into romantic dreams that are doomed to fade and die and be repeated with new actors.

We reap what we sow. Divorce is the fruit of ignorance about our true nature. It is the harvest of ignorance. We cannot teach our children what we do not know. If we do not understand human sexuality and psychology, we cannot protect our young people from perpetuating the cycle of broken homes. We rush to buy our daughters elaborate wedding gowns and stage huge wedding parties. We feel like the bad fairy if we do not greet every engagement as a marvelous possibility, not to be questioned or probed. The minute two young people tell us they are getting married, we drop our judgment at the door and begin to ooh and aah.

In this culture of bad marriages, divorce is a good idea more often than it is a bad idea. But it is nearly always a bad idea for the children. The child nearly always sees it as a fault of his own. He thinks he has failed because his parents do not live together. He thinks he has not been good enough to deserve the American dream of an intact family. This seems to be true even when the lost parent was abusive or alcoholic. All around him the child sees images of families with both mothers and fathers, and it makes him feel impoverished if he has only half this loaf.

Perhaps there is nothing we can do about this. Perhaps we have to muddle along as we have been doing. Making messes of our lives and then cleaning them up as best we can.

~ ~ ~

Years ago, Margaret Mead figured out a plan to lower our divorce rate and keep us from damaging our children. She posited a system of marriages. Any two grown people could apply for a license to be married or to cohabit. If the relationship was successful over a period of time, perhaps two to five years, then they could apply for a second license that would allow them to have a child together.

God knows, I do not want government meddling in the private lives of citizens, but at least we should try to teach young people not to have children until they have achieved a stable home. This means we must fight against nature. Nature doesn't care about quality. Nature has cast its lot with quantity.

The young people of the middle class who have access to reliable birth-control methods seem to be working out a system not unlike the one Margaret Mead proposed. They have a series of cohabitations, and, if one sticks for a long period of time, they get married and produce one or maybe two offspring. Sometimes these arrangements continue to work after the child is born. Sometimes they don't.

I have thought about these matters for years, trying to understand my own failed marriages and the harm divorce wreaked on my sons. I took them away from their father and tried to keep them from him. I was so young I believed they belonged only to me. They had come from my body. I had risked my life to have them. It was impossible for me to think their father had any right to them. Now they are older and have divorces and broken homes of their own. Women have borne children for them and used the children to manipulate them. Women have taken their children from them and made them beg to see them. Because of this, they look at their father with new eyes and commiserate with him. I am glad that time and experience have partially healed a cruelty I thought I had a right to inflict.

I do not know how broken homes and divorces will be stopped. I know that knowledge is our only weapon. We must teach our children the history of our own divorces. We must warn them and beg them to be wiser than we were. We must do whatever is in our power to convince them not to marry until they are old enough to know themselves. How old is that? Thirty for some, forty for others, never for a few.

I am asked all the time about how an artist can balance a family and work. And the truthful answer is that I do not know an artist of great or unusual talent who is married. I will revise that to say an artist of great or unusual talent who uses that talent fully. There is no room in the life of an artist for a husband or a wife or a normal family life. The hours an artist has to spend mulling around in solitude leave no time for the ordinary friendliness and courtesy that a happy marriage demands.

A happy marriage? I am so cynical I really cannot think of one. I know people who are married who have cut deals that allow them to live in relative peace with each other but I don't know any marriages that seem to be delivering much happiness. Perhaps marriage was never supposed to make us happy. Perhaps it is just the price we have to pay to reproduce and make a nest.

The worst thing about divorce is how long it takes to achieve it. It takes as long to decathect as it did to create the problem. For every romantic thought you had about the man or woman to whom you were married, you must now add a cynical, mean, ugly thought. For every time you decided he was Prince Charming, you must now decide he is Evil Incarnate. For every rapturous account of his virtues you gave your friends, you must now add a general account of his impossibility as a spouse.

Spouse: there's a word to make one shudder. From the term, espousal, which means to promise. For every ill-thought-out promise, you must add the legal fine print. Thank goodness for sofas and jointly owned automobiles. As soon as the argument can degenerate into a battle over property, the personal emotional ground can begin to be abandoned.

How ugly all this seems to us while we are going through it. How terrible we feel to be walking around thinking dark thoughts about someone we used to *sleep with*. Just when we think we are making some progress, we run into the person we are divorcing at the grocery store. "Ill met by moonlight, Proud Titania," Oberon says to his queen in Shakespeare's *A Midsummer Night's Dream.* He has come upon her in the forest, where she is dancing with her fairies and elves. She has with her a young boy, the possession of whom is the cause of her dissension with Oberon. Their conversation begins with jealousy, moves on to Titania's blaming Oberon for everything that's wrong with the world, and ends with his throwing the blame back onto her. Especially with a subject as dark as divorce, it is good to stop and drink from the hands of a master.

> *Titania:*
> *These are the forgeries of jealousy;*
> *And never, since the middle summer's spring,*
> *Met we on hill, in dale, forest, or mead,*
> *By paved fountain or by rushy brook,*
> *Or in the beached margent of the sea.*
> *To dance our ringlets to the whistling wind,*
> *But with thy brawls thou hast disturb'd our sport.*
> *Therefore the winds, piping to us in vain,*
> *As in revenge, have suck'd up from the sea*
> *Contagious fogs; which, falling in the land,*
> *Hath every pelting river made so proud*
> *That they have overborne their continents.*
> *The ox hath therefore stretch'd his yoke in vain,*
> *The ploughman lost his sweat, and the green corn*
> *Hath rotted ere his youth attain'd a beard.*
> *The fold stands empty in the drowned field,*
> *And crows are fatted with the murrion flock;*
> *The nine men's morris if fill'd up with mud,*
> *And the quaint mazes in the wanton green,*
> *For lack of tread, are undistinguishable.*
> *The human mortals want their winter here;*
> *No night is now with hymn or carol blest.*
> *Therefore the moon (the governess of floods),*

Pale in her anger, washes all the air,
That rheumatic diseases do abound.
And thorough this distemperature, we see
The seasons alter; hoary-headed frosts
Fall in the fresh lap of the crimson rose,
And on old Hiems' thin and icy crown,
An odorous chaplet of sweet summer buds
Is, as in mockery set; the spring, the summer,
The childing autumn, angry winter, change
Their wonted liveries; and the mazed world,
By their increase, now knows not which is which.
And this same progeny of evils comes
From our debate, from our dissension;
We are their parents and original.

Who has ever written a more perfect description of the way the injured party feels when a marriage has broken up? The winds have sucked up from the sea contagious fogs. Rivers have overborne their continents. The seasons have changed places. Hoary-headed frosts fall in the fresh lap of the crimson rose . . . And this same progeny of evils comes from our debate, from our dissension. . . .

Sometimes divorces are caused by children. Even a marriage that was consummated in the hope of having children may break down under the pressure of caring for and supporting the endless and expensive needs of children. Modern, educated women sometimes find the wear and tear of taking care of small children twenty-four hours a day is more than they bargained for.

I know of marriages that are breaking down because the children have become rebellious teenagers. The parents feel cheated. They have given their lives and the sweat of their brows for those ungrateful creatures. They feel they have wasted their lives. Perhaps they have.

Platitudes or shaky moral ground will not save us now. We have big problems in this culture. And all problems begin in infancy, in the home, in the mother-child relationship, and in the force field we call family.

Some people make better mothers than others do. Some men make better fathers. This doesn't mean that some men and women are better than others, just that they are more temperamentally suited to the job of raising children. Where does this lead us?

One thing I know is that it is a bad idea to marry someone who had bad parents. If they hated their mother, if they were hated by their mother or father, your marriage will pay for it in ways both obvious and subtle. When the chips are down, when someone is sick or loses their job or gets scared, the old patterns will kick in and he will treat you the way he treated his mother or the way she treated him. If she yelled at him and compared him to others and blamed him for her own shortcomings, this is the treatment you will receive. If she expected to be constantly admired and rewarded, he will expect that. And this is just the problem with his (or her) mother. Before we even get to the father.

Divorces are also caused by people outgrowing each other or outgrowing the need for the marriage they have made. Sometimes marriages are broken down by events: the death or sickness of a child, the sickness or disability of one of the partners, sudden wealth, sudden poverty, all the things that the marriage ceremony in *The Book of Common Prayer* warned against. For richer, for poorer, for better, for worse, in sickness and in health, and forsaking all others . . .

The world that such marriages were made for no longer exists in the middle-class life of the United States. We *don't* depend on each other for food, clothing, housing, nursing, and are left depending on each other for company and emotional support. Most of the married people I know go to their friends for fun and gossip and long walks where everyone says exactly what they think.

Also, we live much longer than the people who wrote the ceremonies in the prayer books of our various religions. We don't want to forsake all others. We leave our troubled houses where children are sick and bills must be paid and travel to our offices where there are bright, well-dressed, good-natured people of the opposite sex, and we forsake. Oh, do we forsake! If not in physical ways, then in emotional ways, which are equally damaging to the marriages we left behind that morning.

We live so long we have time for two or three major careers, two or three or more transformations. We become someone new and the person we are married to feels betrayed. They have been betrayed. The person they married has ceased to exist and they feel cheated.

The only hope I can see for the unhappiness of divorce is knowing that it is better than a bad marriage. The unhappiness of divorce ends, in time, for healthy people. Healthy people refuse to stay unhappy. Sooner or later they wake up and decide to be happy again. They lose weight and start exercising. They dye their hair or get a toupee. They buy a red dress and go to a party and start flirting. They redecorate their living quarters. They get out their address books and start looking for old lovers to recycle.

Life goes on. They look back on their marriage and wonder who that person was who inhabited that troubled world. Time, the old healer, has erased the footsteps that led them to the altar and the divorce court.

The Wine Dark Sea

I'M SICK OF EVERYONE ELSE HAVING ALL THE FUN TALKING about menopause. I want to get my oar in. I went through menopause. My experience is just as good as anyone else's. Here's what happens. You stop menstruating. Blood stops running out of your body six days a month. You stop ruining all your silk underpants. You stop having to borrow Tampax from strangers in public restrooms during ball games and ballets and movies. (The first one I borrowed was in a movie theatre in Harrisburg, Illinois. I was thirteen and it was a Kotex since Tampax hadn't been invented yet.)

Sometimes you can't borrow one. Sometimes you have to stuff your underpants full of Kleenex or your handkerchief or a sock. Then you slink home full of shame.

Back to the menopause. First you don't menstruate every month. You menstruate some months and not others. This is okay except that you think you're pregnant all the time. I made a lot of money off that experience by writing a book about a woman who has a baby when she is forty-four. It is called *The Annunciation* and has sold about three hundred thousand copies in the last twelve years.

The other thing that happens is that you have hot flashes. This is very exciting if you let it be. You are walking across a room minding your own business and suddenly you are consumed by heat. Your body heats up to about a hundred and four. This happens in seconds. You break out in a sweat. Then the heat passes and only the sweat remains. You have been reminded of mortality and death and where you are in space and time. You are in the universe of process and decay, of atoms and particles and human biology, that frail and delicate phenomena to end all phenomena.

Take that excitement into your soul. Understand who and where and what you are. You are awake now, not in the stupor in which most of us live our lives. Rilke said it is as though our life is a room but as we grow older we only inhabit a small part of the room, pacing up and down before a window, tracing and retracing our steps. He said, *"We must accept our experience as vastly as we possibly can; everything, even the unprecedented, must be possible within it."*

Of course, for this you need courage and the strength to be alone with your own mortality. You have to forget what the outside world thinks of you. You have to push aside the trashy notions of our culture. You have to remember mountains and rivers and the motions of planets. You have to remember snow and streams and your life in the womb. You have to bend down to your own unimaginable curiosity, to the dazzling impossibility of being here, in this form, on this earth, with this day before you to be lived. You have to grow up.

There is always a lot of free-floating anxiety in any psyche and it will latch onto anything it can. Menopause has always been fertile ground for anxiety. Don't give in to this syndrome.

Take estrogen if you can. Or don't take it. Exercise at least an hour a day. Hard, intense exercise, long walks or bicycle rides, aerobics or dance classes. Make exercise a priority. Use it as a shield against fear. Eat intelligently, drink bottled water, take vitamins, sit in meditation, listen to music, turn off the television set. Don't be afraid. The best is yet to come. These are the high passes where the air gets thin and the light becomes translucent.

"Keep warm, old man," the boy said. *"Remember we are in September."*

"The month when the big fish come," the old man said. *"Anyone can be a fisherman in May."**

---

* Earnest Hemingway, *The Old Man and the Sea*

Blessings

NOW THAT I AM GROWING OLD I AM BEGINNING TO HAVE WON-
derful dreams. I dream that I am doing things I can no longer do
in my waking life, making love to interesting and exotic men, playing highly competitive tennis with exciting opponents on perfectly
groomed courts in perfect weather, ice skating down long halls in my
mansion. In the ice skating dream a handsome man and I are trying
out the halls for the young people and the children. We are deciding
how slick the halls should be and how thick to make the ice. This is
all easily controlled by a thermostat on a wall in the mansion kitchen.
There are ten or twelve young people in the house, ranging from ten
or twelve years old to seventeen. In another room are toddlers with
their nurses and their mothers but they are playing other games and
we are not sure we will let them on the ice. "Hey," I tell the man.
"I'm not making this ice too slick. After all, if they hurt themselves
we're the ones who will have to take care of them."

"Don't want to spoil the fun," he agrees and smiles. He's falling in
love with me, I know. With my intelligence and good humor, with
my ability to organize and make decisions. It's my mansion, after all.
The rest of them are here at my invitation.

My dreams are like television situation comedies. They are arranged
into scenes which move and blend into other scenes. Old characters
remain and new ones are introduced. In the love scenes the men who
loved me are my old husbands but decked out in new personalities.
One night my lover was a beautiful American Indian with a modern

personality. There is no shame or hurry in these love scenes. We talk it over with intelligence. We discuss possible problems that might arise, harm to other people or ourselves, how much emotional weight we should invest in the matter. Sometimes we proceed, sometimes we decide it's not worth the risk. No one gets hurt in any way. It is passionate but not very. It is like a business transaction or a decision made in a psychoanalyst's office.

The decisions made in these intelligent, lifelike dreams are all based on what is best for the young people who are in our care. In the dreams I am the alpha female, there are one or two alpha males helping me and we have young children in our care. There seems to hang over the dreams a sense of impending disaster which we constantly monitor. We do not tell the young people about it. It is as if we know there is a hurricane or storm coming and we keep the young near us without letting them be aware of the danger. We are not worried about this approaching storm but neither do we forget it.

I think this is the heaven men have dreamed of. A quiet world with work to do for beautiful young people who look at you with trusting eyes. No matter what I am doing in the dreams, playing tennis, ice skating, making love, I think of myself as a guardian, as someone who is the teacher.

Here's where the heavenly part comes in. I know I am competent to care for these children. I have no doubt that I will be able to keep them safe. The men who help me are intelligent and thoughtful. There is no way we will make the ice too slick or deep. There is no way the approaching storm will batter down the walls of the fortress we are minding. We go for long walks into the grounds and woods outside the mansion. We tuck the children into safe beds. I patrol the halls while I'm sleeping. I can wake up early if I like or I can go on sleeping.

If this is old age then I adore being sixty-four years old and believe sixty-five is going to be even better. Perhaps then I'll dream of Medicare and Social Security. Getting checks in the mail from the federal government. Intelligent, good-looking men will call me up and tell me not to send any more money to the I.R.S. "Time to cash in now," the agent will say. "Thank you, officer," I will answer. I'll get into my convertible and drive off with my good-looking companion. We'll pop open a can of Ensure and drive off into a sunset.

When I Worry I Run As Fast As I Can

———————————◄❯►———————————

THE GREATEST LESSON I EVER LEARNED WAS TAUGHT TO ME every day as a child but didn't sink in until I was in my early thirties. My father had been a professional baseball player until I was born and he was forced to settle down and make a living as a contractor and an engineer.

Every day of my life as a child I was being taught to play sports. I was an afterthought in these lessons to some extent because my father had more luck teaching sports to my brothers. My brothers worshipped him and would dare anything and practice endlessly in order to please him. It took more coaching to get me to strap roller skates onto my feet and agree to fall off two more times before I got the feel and learned to love speed. But I could not bear to be left out so if it was daylight and we weren't in school we were outside learning to pit our bodies against baseball, basketball, roller skating, scooters, stilts, push-up bars, football, ice skating, rope climbing, tree climbing, camping, hunting, bow and arrow practice, and, most importantly to my father, bicycle riding and horseback riding. I didn't last long in the hunting department. They quit taking me on those expeditions after I shot at a bird when I was behind them early one morning.

I also remember races, running as hard as I could across pastures and down broken sidewalks. When I was in grade school and junior high I swam on swimming teams until I became so saturated with chlorine my red hair would turn greenish blond. In the ninth grade I gave up many of my sports activities for cheerleading, which was not very good exercise in the nineteen forties and nineteen fifties.

The thing I longed to do that was not available to girls back then was be on a track team. Part of my mind was relieved not to have to jump over hurdles. I am not very tall and the times I tried hurdle jumping were not successful. So I left track events to my brothers and became less and less athletic as my high school years went by. I was a great reader and read four or five books a week, besides my schoolwork. This worried my father greatly. He was always yelling at my mother, "Get that girl out into the sunshine. Don't let her sit up there all day reading a book."

It was good advice, but I didn't know it then. It was tantamount to allowing children in this age to sit in front of a television set or computer all day and fill their minds with fantasies and fiction.

The real world is out there. The human body needs to move, to spread its wings and stretch out and twist and turn and be challenged.

By the time I was a high school junior I had pretty much lost all my real sports. I still swam like a demon for as long as I could anytime I was in or near a body of water and I always loved to ride bicycles but there were no organized sports in my life. Also, I was getting chubby. Not fat, but chubby enough to scare my mother into taking me to the doctor to get some diet pills.

I took a lot of diet pills between the time I was nineteen and the time I fell down a set of stairs when I was thirty-two.

Fortunately for me and my friends it became very difficult to get diet pills. Doctors would only give you a few at a time.

Here's the main thing. Here's the thing I didn't know. You cannot stop being even mildly chubby by taking diet pills and trying to starve yourself. The only way you can lose weight is by constant, hard, aerobic exercise and learning to control the sugar and carbohydrates in your diet.

When I was thirty-two years old my best friend told me that her brother was *running*. He was a handsome, much-admired man in

New Orleans who had given up making money to save the environment. He had been on the cover of *Time* magazine. We adored him. Even my hardworking lawyer husband adored him. Anything Dick Bambaugh, Junior, decided to do had the rest of us watching and applauding.

"He's running," she repeated. "And he thinks we should too. He thinks we are nuts to keep going on these stupid diets. He said he'd teach us how to run."

"Where does he go running?" I asked. "Where does he do it?"

"He runs on top of the levee," she answered. "He runs from the power relay station at the end of Carrollton Avenue to Ochsner's Clinic. It's a long way. He said all we needed to do was run one mile a day to begin with."

"What does he wear?" I asked.

"Well, he runs in his combat boots and some heavy clothes to make himself sweat but he said we could just run in our tennis clothes."

"What else did he say?"

"He said go down to the athletic store on Carrollton and tell them we want some running shoes and running socks. Then he said to just go out and put one foot down in front of the other faster than a walk."

"I'll try it," I said. "I'll do anything to get this fat off my waist."

The next morning, as soon as our children were in school, Bonnie and I went to the store and bought two pairs of boy's running shoes and put them on and went up on top of the Carrollton Avenue levee and started running. I had watched my brothers run track all my life. I knew what to do. I knew how to run. Every human being knows how to run.

The first day we managed somehow or other to run about three-fourths of a mile by stopping when we got out of breath. It was an epiphany to me to see how easily I was winded. I knew all about being winded and about how the body makes hemoglobin in the blood to make you stronger if you force it to need hemoglobin.

"Dick said if we ran from the pumping station to the curve at Maple Street we would have gone a mile," Bonnie said.

"Tomorrow we'll go that far," I said. It was already clear to both of us that there would be no going back now that we had started. If the famous and admired Dick Bambaugh was running we were running too.

It was an amazing next couple of months. We ran every day. Sometimes we ran in the rain if it wasn't falling too hard. We got better shoes. We learned what to wear in different weathers. We started begging people to come and run with us. We dragged my poor hardworking husband away from his papers and made him run. He had rowed single sculls at Exeter and Harvard. He had been an athlete. He took to it as we did.

I remember the day we ran a mile without stopping as if it were yesterday. Breathless and excited we hugged each other and turned around and started running back.

I remember the first time I ran six miles, the first time I ran nine miles, the first time I ran eighteen miles ALL THE WAY AROUND THE PARK THREE TIMES AND THEN DOWN TO THE LEVEE AND ALL THE WAY TO OCHSNER'S CLINIC.

I remember the morning I drove alone to Covington, Louisiana, and ran twenty-six miles across the causeway and won my New Orleans Marathon medal.

All that time and until now I have never been chubby again. I sometimes gain five or six pounds but I have never stopped running or doing something equally aerobic every day of my life. I am the strongest and most fit seventy-three-year-old in any group of people where I find myself. I don't need facelifts or tummy tucks. I am a physical human being and every day of my life, with a few hated exceptions, I do something that is the equivalent of running at least three miles.

Many times in the last few years that means walking very fast on a treadmill raised to the level of a steep hill.

Exercise is the meat and bread of my existence. The single most important thing I do and the thing on which my mental and physical health depend.

In all these years, between thirty-two and seventy-three, I have had small pieces of time when I forgot that exercise is the basis of mental and physical health but they are small pieces of time and I always come back to my better angels.

I want so much to get other people to do this. I know many people have handicaps that keep them from running but there are so many muscles in the body. Remember Dick Bambaugh, my exercise hero. Remember my daddy. Get those children off of those couches and teach them some sports. Get yourself off of those couches and save your lives. I'll be thinking of you. I'll be sending you all my best and most aerobic wishes.

ADDENDA, JANUARY 2015

I will be eighty years old in February. I still exercise an hour and a half every day and I still love it and I'm still healthy and strong and thinner than I've ever been in my life. It gets more difficult to find ways to get out of breath occasionally but I find them. WHATEVER IT TAKES. That's my motto and my creed. I don't mind being old but I'm damned if I'm going to become an invalid. Exercise works. And it's never too late to start.

Pollen, Part I

———————

ALLERGY CLINICS ARE TURNING OUT TO BE THE PICKUP BARS OF the nineties. The one to which I go is in a brick building near a junior high school. There is soft Christian music playing in the room where you sign in for your shots. It is early morning. Each person comes in the door and signs his or her name on an extremely small line. Beside most of the names it says SHOT. We are here to be desensitized to our environment. If you view allergy attacks, or being symptomatic, as we call it in the trade, as a full glass of water, then you can imagine desensitization as an attempt to slowly empty the glass. In the end, if all goes well, you will be back where you started, with a nice clean glass shining on your shelf. Your nose will stop running, your eyes will open, and you will be able to get your work done and live and eat and so forth. Yet another victory in the kitchen of life.

I have come to join this crusade. Every Wednesday I jump out of bed and throw on my clothes and drive down to get my shot. After the sign-in, you wait a short time in the outer office, which more or less resembles the deck of a cruise ship. Instead of the sea you are facing a wall of glass panels behind which the nurses are sorting folders, talking on telephones and moving briskly to the inspirational music. It is eight o'clock in the morning. I am dressed in pale green silk slacks, Birkenstocks with Chanel toenail polish, and a short-sleeved white shirt I ordered from a Lands' End catalogue.

I'm a grown woman. I'm not afraid of shots. From the back room a small boy screams. A long, murderous, enraged scream. He screams again. The nurses look down at their work. They have steeled themselves to children's tantrums. After three weeks I have figured something out. The roll of fat on my upper arms has been there all along for a purpose. The reason I feel no need to scream when I get my shot is that I have this lovely roll of passionless fat to absorb the antigens. There is so little nerve tissue in that part of the arm, as any woman knows who has ever tried to exercise it away, that all I feel is a mild soreness. This is almost welcome as it tells me some of the antigens are attempting to escape the fat and make their way into my bloodstream, where, hopefully, my T cells will identify the intruders and mount appropriate defenses, thereby saving the lining of my nose and ears from going into citizen's arrest and overreacting. So much for science.

Experience is knowledge and so I have agreed to come down here every Wednesday for a year and stick out my arm and let them inject me with antigens made from seven different kinds of mold and several grasses and ragweed pollen. Fifty-two shots. If this doesn't work I will have to move to the Virgin Islands and live on a sailboat. As it is, I can't breathe freely in the place where I live and work, so I have decided it's worth a shot. Or 52 shots or 104 or 208 shots. I am into this now. I am committed.

This morning the tune in the outer waiting room is "A Mighty Fortress Is Our God," played in ragtime. I could ask them to turn the music down, as I am trying to read *Smilla's Sense of Show* by Peter Hoeg and have just gotten to the scary part where Smilla boards the icebreaker bound for Greenland, but I asked them to turn it down last week and I don't want to turn into a pest. Last week I was reading *The Power of One* by Bryce Courtenay and was at the part where they wrench the hero from his beloved mammy and ship him off to an Afrikaans boarding school. The reason I love to read books by foreign writers is that they have no sense of political correctness and there are heroes and villains of every age, sex, color, and race and it's easy to tell the good guys from the bad ones. Besides, I am trying to learn how to plot.

Fortunately there are no long waits in Dr. Hutson's allergy clinic. She runs this place like IBM. She is not giving any little children or skittish women writers time to change their minds and slip out the door, something I did at a different allergy clinic two years ago. I got all the way to the waiting room, then bolted.

Within minutes I am called to go down a wide white hall to a small examining room equipped with comfortable chairs and books on hidden food allergies and a cheerful red examining table where I imagine the smaller patients sit to get their shots. A nurse attaches my folder to the door and tells me Dr. Hutson will be there soon. I pick up the food allergy book and begin to read a list of suspect foods. It's pretty much a list of the things I routinely eat. Milk, eggs, wheat, coffee, chocolate, corn, strawberries, shellfish, peanuts. Lucky for me, I inhale my allergens. I begin to feel very lucky reading that book. What if I were being made sick by all my favorite foods as well as the air I breathe?

I settle into a meditative state. I see smokestacks from paper mills, the exhaust pipes of automobiles, clear-cut forests, plastics factories, vats of chemicals, the wheat and corn fields of the Midwest, feeding lots for pork, beef, and poultry, all the vast network of farmers and manufacturers who produce the things that make my life a paradise of products, goods and services, Would I go back to living in the woods? Not on your life.

The door opens and the divine Dr. Hutson enters the room. I love her. I love her pretty blue dress and her crisp white lab coat and her curly white hair and her dedication and her kindness. I have put myself in her hands. "Bring on the shot," I say. "I can't wait."

A child screams in a far room. Then screams again. "No, no, no, no, no," he screams.

"No fat on his upper arm," I say. "I have a friend who teaches children with learning disabilities. She says 80 percent of them don't have anything wrong with their brains. They have allergies and can't think straight for the mucus in their little upper respiratory systems."

"I know," Dr. Hutson says.

"So does it really hurt them very much, what with no fat?"

"I don't think so."

"The imagination is a powerful God."

"That it is," she agrees.

We proceed to the back half and Dr. Hutson puts my chart in the proper slot and I stick out my arm and the nurse injects me with the antigens. She hands me a kitchen timer and I join my fellow allergy-sufferers in the second waiting room. Each patient has a timer and a book or magazine. It occurs to me that maybe this is all part of a larger scheme to keep the American public literate. As in airplanes and airports, there is nothing to do in this room but read. The chairs are arranged in two concentric circles with plenty of room in between the circles. It seems to be de rigueur to be silent but the brighter-looking patients are checking each other out. There is a well-dressed elderly couple sitting side by side and reading *Forbes* and *Vogue*. There is an Indian woman with a child who seems to have Down's syndrome. She is a really lovely little girl and is standing on her chair watching me. There is a small blond child reading an *Easy Reader* in hushed tones to her mother and alternately rubbing her arm and whimpering. I sit across from her and pretend to be fascinated by her reading. She suppresses a smile, raises her voice an infinitesimal amount and sits up straighter.

There is a teenage boy reading *Time* and a farmer in his work clothes. We are joined by the small boy who was screaming while I talked to the doctor. He is all smiles now, holding his father's hand and sucking a red lollipop.

The music is not as loud back here. I settle down with my book. The air conditioner hums. I am on a cruise ship. It is Wednesday morning in the real world and there is work to be done, but not in Dr. Hutson's back waiting room. All I have to do is read my book and think about the huge breakfast I'm going to buy myself as soon as this is over.

A handsome man in a blue-and-white polo shirt sits down beside me. He sets his timer near mine and whispers, "This is my first time. How about you?"

"It's my third. I think it's a reasonably sound theory. I think it's going to cure me."

"I've read that book. It's extraordinary, don't you think?"

"I've read it twice. The British translation and the American translation. They translated it twice. No one knows why. I suppose because the measurements were in the metric system. So what are you in for?"

"Molds and pollen and dust. How about you?"

"The same. When this buzzer goes off I'm going down to Pete's Grill and eat waffles and bacon and scrambled eggs. Come and join me. If this is your first shot, you should celebrate."

"Maybe I will. I didn't have time to eat. I barely got here through the traffic."

"Come on over. I want to talk to everyone who's doing this. I'm obsessed with it. It's all I think about."

"I'll meet you there." He smiles a grand, conspiratorial smile at me. This is not sexual. We are just two people deciding to take a chance one morning. Besides, he reminds me of the father of my children, whom I married years ago for his body.

My buzzer goes off. I take it to the nurse's station and stick out my arm to have my shot checked. "Is it swollen?" I ask. "Is it red?"

"To tell the truth I can't even see where the needle went in," she answers.

I go to the checkout desk in the front waiting room. "The Church's One Foundation" is being played in waltz time by an enthusiastic symphony orchestra. I turn in my chart. I walk out into the bright sunshine and problematic air of the place where I live. I hum a few bars of the hymn the way it is played in Episcopal churches. I strike off in the direction of the restaurant. There is nothing to fear, I tell myself. I am not sick. I have started my shots. There is nothing wrong with me that the genius of my fellow man can't fix.

Pollen, Part II

─────────────

I HAVE NEVER IMAGINED MYSELF BEING SICK OR ILL. I HAVE always believed I have a huge store of magnificent health stored up against all disaster.

When I was young I recovered from childhood illnesses with determination and swiftness. Several times in my teenage years I was carried out of my mother's house on a stretcher with pneumonia caused by sinus infections but I remember nothing about the illnesses until I was being carried down the stairs and put into the ambulances and given the pleasure of imagining the town's shock as they heard me roaring by. Both of these hospitalizations occurred in a small town in the vicinity of Nashville, Tennessee, where we lived for several years during my father's pursuit of a million dollars. He made the million dollars, by the way, and spent the rest of his life giving it to charities and other people. He loved giving money away to family and friends and other people. No one ever had to ask. He saw needs and filled them.

It was many years after those ambulance rides before I had another sinus attack of enough severity to put me to bed. My third husband and I had rented an upstairs apartment on State Street in uptown New Orleans while we renovated a house we had bought. There was a swimming pool beneath our living quarters and I now know this was my first encounter with pernicious mold in housing.

An ear, nose, and throat doctor cured that sickness by putting some sort of "hot wires" through my sinus cavities and I forgot about upper respiratory problems for awhile. My main memory of that attack is when my cousin returned from China bringing me a glamorous kimono made of royal blue silk. I lent the kimono to a young painter named Ginny Stanford and she painted it on several portrait customers. She grew up to paint a gorgeous official portrait of Hillary Clinton, which hangs in the White House, has portraits in the National Gallery of Art in Washington, D. C., and has fulfilled the promise her friends recognized early in her career. I used her paintings of our friends as covers for many of my books.

Several years went by and I forgot about upper respiratory problems and sinus cavities. Then I moved to Fayetteville, Arkansas, in the Ozark Mountains, on exactly the same latitude as Nashville, Tennessee, and, like Nashville, situated in the middle of beautiful tree-covered hills.

The first spring I lived in Fayetteville I thought I was catching recurrent colds from the other students in the writing program, where I was attempting to learn how to publish my poems and stories.

I noted the "colds" but I didn't treat them or worry about them. I was too entranced with the absolute beauty of watching trees and spring flowers turn the black and gray of winter into a fairyland. Redbuds, dogwoods, forsythia, oak, pine, hickory, cherry, apple, elm, maple, and locust trees were flowering and leafing in such elegant processions and with such perfect timing that I would walk about all day thinking of William Wordsworth and Robert Frost and not even trying to turn my joy into words.

As much poetry as I was writing every day I could not begin to make poems out of the wonder of watching a real spring develop. I had been in New Orleans for eleven years where everything is always leafed and blossoming. In Fayetteville I was watching the tiniest of buds develop into leaves and bloom, the beginning buds so like the human hand that there is nothing else to say after you say that.

"A flower of feathers or a winged branch," Pedro Calderon de la Barca had written many centuries before. It was a description of a bird in flight but it worked for what I was watching on the trees.

~ ~ ~

Besides the trees and flowers, the hyacinths, daffodils, jonquils, violets, dandelions, lilies of the valley, and tulips, there was the weather, banks of beautiful clouds, rainstorms, thunderstorms, threats of tornadoes. That spring had it all for a pilgrim who had been raised in the temperate zones and returned after long exile to the splendor of seasons. There were days of downpours that made every hill a waterfall and, for once in the Ozarks, no untimely frosts to kill the buds.

When I left in late April to go back to New Orleans I packed my Rambler station wagon, then went out into the yard to have one last inspection of the hickory trees near the sidewalk. There was a delicate leafing slowly evolving on them. Tiny buds that turned into pale green hands, then darker green, then gold.

I remember thinking, well, at least I might get rid of these endless colds, but I can't bear to be gone when these bright green flowers turn into leaves.

The following year I moved to Fayetteville for good. I kept a house in New Orleans for awhile but Fayetteville had become my home. It was the place where I liked to write, the place where the muse came to me and stayed with me and brought me blessings and brought me luck.

It was six or seven years later before I gave in to the pleadings of my friends and went to a physician to see if, by some weird turn of fate, I could have "allergies." I barely knew what the word meant. I thought it was some sort of weakness or shameful defect that could not possibly apply to me.

Sixteen years later I am a full-fledged chronic sinus sufferer, proud to be a survivor of full-fledged allergic reactions to pollen, mold, dust, and every gorgeous tree and plant known to man. I take allergy shots. I inhale cortisone through my nose and suck it down into my lungs. I take Advair and Flonase and Zyrtec and, when the pollen count gets high enough, I take prednisone and, God forbid, Sudafed.

~ ~ ~

I am in a bad mood when I ingest and inhale these medicines. Remember, I am an enormously healthy person who has never been sick in my life and I think some mistake has been made. Possibly, I have overlooked a variable, and, as soon as I find it, this will all be over.

I have a young friend who likes to tell me that no matter how much I understand this illness, it will not make it go away. She wants me to accept these allergies as part of the inevitable tragic nature of "life in the body." Sometimes I pretend to see the wisdom of her counsel, but deep down inside I know it is not true. I can conquer this aberration. After all I haven't even tried Singulair yet. I like knowing I have Singulair waiting in the wings in case the star falls out during a performance.

Meanwhile I know two things for certain. I will never stop adoring spring and its gifts and beauties. And I will never stop knowing that most of my life is lived with hope and promise and a clear head.

A few months on Sudafed is a humbling experience but it is a small price to pay for flowering and blossoming and blooming.

MARCH 26, 2007

UPDATE, OCTOBER 16, 2010

I have made a discovery about allergies that may be of use to other sufferers. In June of 2009 a young married couple I know went to a clinic in the Swiss Alps to be treated for Lyme disease. It is an alternative medicine clinic called Paracelsus.

The day they got home from Switzerland they begged me to come over to their house and talk to them about what they had learned. They were glowing with good health and happiness. They felt they had made their first real assault on the disease that had been plaguing their lives for five years.

The heart of the treatment was a detoxification diet which rids your body of primary allergies you developed as a child and are unaware of having. These primary allergies are a constant low-grade drain on the immune system and make things like allergies and asthma much worse.

I took the book my friends had brought me and went home and went on the diet. It is easy to do. You remove all foods from your diet that have ever been known to cause allergies in anyone. What is left is a diet of steamed vegetables, vegetable soup, grapefruits, apples, pecans, cashews, broiled fish, salads, goat cheese, cashew butter on Spelt bread toast, eggs, and, especially, a lot of things to eat that I had not tasted in years. Avocado, baked potatoes, one piece of dark chocolate every day.

I went on the three-week diet religiously. I had been suffering spring allergies so badly I could not work.

In two days I began to feel like a different person. I lost five pounds without ever feeling hungry. My head cleared. I stopped taking allergy medicines, except for Astelin Nose Spray.

I stayed on the crucial beginning diet for four weeks. Then I went on the maintenance diet which adds foods slowly and carefully.

If my allergies get bad I go immediately back onto the beginning diet. This has worked wonders for my allergies and my energy levels and my general health.

I learned from the diet that I am allergic to wheat bread and cereals, which have always been the main thing I like to eat. I had already eliminated dairy products from my diet.

My allergies are not a problem for me anymore. I stopped eating everything that made them worse, especially things that contain gluten, a word I later learned.

Allergies have many causes all mixed together. Perhaps my discovery will be of use to some of my readers. My editor thinks I should take this part out of this essay but if it stops one person from having to resort to Sudafed it's worth it to me.

The Joy of Swimming

MY REVIVED LOVE OF THE AUSTRALIAN CRAWL BEGAN AS A LAST resort. A last resort is exactly that, "something to which or someone to whom one looks for help; a source of aid or refuge."

I am a short, redheaded Pisces, how fitting that my last resort should be water. All my life I have loved getting wet, wanted to wade or jump into any body of water, from bathtubs to lakes or rivers or cow ponds. I have viewed any floatable device as a way to save drowning people or go out deeper into water. (I took Red Cross lifesaver lessons in my early teens.) I have wanted any boat I ever saw or read about, from Huckleberry Finn's raft to fishing boats tied to the pier in front of my grandmother's house. Later, I owned a sailboat in the British Virgin Islands. I never loved motorboats as they make too much noise. My relationship with water is quieter and more spiritual than that. Besides, in my youth most motors didn't work most of the time. I liked paddles. You can count on a paddle.

When I was four years old my father began to teach me to put my face down in the bath water and breathe out air. He was teaching me to swim all winter while we waited for spring. I have no fear of drowning because my parents were teaching me to swim and preaching water safety tips even before the Red Cross instructors took over.

To this day if I walk up to a swimming pool the first thing I notice is the white lifesaving ring. It lifts my heart to see one anywhere.

Is my love of water instinct or learned behavior? I think about that every morning when I open the door to the glass house which covers my outrageously expensive lap pool and walk around the edge to watch the light moving on the water. Then I climb down the ladder and begin to swim my fifty or sixty laps.

We are drawn to water because we lived in it for millions of years before we climbed up on land and started compressing our spinal columns by walking. While swimming the spinal column stretches out and feels wonderful. It is compression of the lumbar spine that caused me to rediscover the joy of swimming and build a ridiculously expensive lap pool.

In the summer of two thousand and eight, at the age of seventy-four, my lower back absolutely wasn't going to let me run or walk long distances or do yoga or Pilates anymore. I had seen it coming. Several times, in the last fifteen years, I had looked out into my large, unused backyard and begun to make my plans. If worst came to worst I could always swim. I would build a long skinny lap pool and swim laps. Someday I might get so old that I couldn't do anything, but not yet, not until I had tried every single thing that man's imagination has made possible.

In the meantime there were exercises I could do on machines at my health club. I could walk half a mile on good days. I could lift weights while lying on my back.

I was searching for a neurosurgeon to operate on my back. I was getting injections from a pain management specialist. I was talking to a young chiropractor who takes care of the athletic teams at the university where I work. I was thinking as hard as I could. This was a problem to be solved and I could solve it.

One morning in late June I took a friend to my health club. She is a beautiful woman who is struggling valiantly to care for her brave dying husband. I wanted to get her out of her house, to remind her to care for herself while she cared for him. "Bring a bathing suit," I said. "There are two Olympic-sized saltwater pools at the club. We might try them out."

"Have you been in them?" she asked.

"No, the water is too cold in the indoor pool and I'm never at the club at the right time to use the outdoor pool. I can't get much sun anymore."

When we got to the club my friend scared me by putting too much weight on the machines she was trying, so I said, "Let's go swimming. The water may be cold but we can try it."

"Let's go," she answered. "What is there to fear? If it's too cold we'll get in the sauna to warm up."

"Have you ever been in a saltwater pool?"

"No, but I've been in the ocean. Not to mention the womb."

Fifteen minutes later Callie and I had on bathing suits and were climbing down a ladder into water that was heated to seventy-nine degrees, not hot enough for ladies our age but bearable. Callie is only sixty-five and is the kind of woman they don't make anymore. She attended the same Episcopal boarding school that polished my mother's perfect manners.

"It's cold," she said. "We'd better start swimming." She struck off down the seventy-five-foot lane with her perfectly coiffed head held out of water, a style of swimming that would break my neck.

I lay down in the water and started doing the old Australian crawl my father taught me years ago. The first six or seven strokes were awkward, then it began to come back to me, all the years of coaching when my father dreamed I might grow up to swim the English Channel. "Elbows, Sister," he would yell. "Use those legs."

I stretched out and began to swim faster. It felt wonderful. For the first time in many months I was exercising without pain. I was getting out of breath without having to pay for it with pain and numbness.

I swam thirteen laps. Callie swam twenty, using the side stroke and the back stroke and her head-above-water crawl.

Early the next morning I went back to the pool alone and swam twenty-two laps. By the end of the week I was swimming twenty-five. By the end of the month I was up to thirty.

I had a goal. I had read in the newspaper that a neurosurgeon at Duke University had operated on Ted Kennedy's brain. The Kennedy family had done my research for me. My publisher in Durham, North Carolina, found the neurosurgeon's name for me and I called and he told me the name of a spinal surgeon on his staff. I flew to Durham, met the surgeon, and made plans to have a minimally invasive decompression of the lumbar spine in September.

I was training for the surgery by swimming. I swam almost every day. My friend Callie, meanwhile, had hired a trainer and was lifting weights for exercise. She was not ready to trade her hairdo for endorphins. Even a saltwater pool has a certain amount of chlorine in the water.

The pool I built is treated with Baquacil, but when I had to swim in pools treated with salt or chlorine I did it, just as I climbed down into the water no matter what the temperature as long as I had to do that.

Being able to walk without pain is worth any price. The joy of moving through water, of getting out of breath, of keeping my blood pressure low, not to mention the Zen pleasures of being immersed in water, far outweigh a momentary discomfort in cool water.

Swimming thirty laps a day was the only exercise I did during the months leading up to my surgery. When I went to the hospital for stress tests to see if I could stand the surgery I passed with flying colors. I was as strong as I had been when I was running six miles a day.

While I was in Durham recuperating from the surgery at Duke the stock market fell two thousand points. I didn't even call my stockbroker. I could walk without pain. It seemed irrelevant that I had lost half my retirement savings.

When I got home from the surgery I called a pool construction company and ordered the pool. I went to the bank and borrowed money for the first time in my life. The pool company came into my yard and cut down four nice trees and tore up all my grass and started building. They built me a sixty-foot-long lap pool that is ten feet wide and covered by a steel-and-glass house.

My hair has already been sacrificed so I cut it even shorter. All my life I have had shoulder-length hair. Now it became shorter and shorter. I love having short hair. It curls all over my head. It almost never has to be fixed or messed with. My students say it makes me look like a character in a Scott Fitzgerald novel. My cousins say it makes me look like my mother.

Meanwhile my back is free from pain, my posture has improved, and my arms and shoulders look better than they have looked in years.

There is something about swimming all alone in cool blue water that is pure Zen. I swim the Australian crawl, slowly at first, then faster and faster. I swim forty to sixty minutes every morning as the sun comes in the windows and makes wonderful patterns on the lining of the pool. Sometimes I take off my swimming suit and feel the water moving the muscles of my arms and legs. I pretend I'm Michael Phelps. I pretend I am a dolphin. I think about my father running along the edge of a pool coaching me. "Elbows, Sister. Let them lift themselves."

I listen to music while I swim. John Coltrane, Beethoven, Bach, the Gypsy Kings, Keith Jarrett, Louis Armstrong.

When I was young I wanted to be the bravest, fastest girl in the world. Now I am the oldest person I know who was ever crazy enough to borrow money from a bank in the middle of an economic crisis.

We swam for millions of years before we walked on land. We swam for nine months before we came out into the air and started screaming. No screaming in the water. No screaming in the beautiful little blue and white pool I built with borrowed money. I'm paying it back as fast as I can.

AUGUST 27, 2009

~ ~ ~

Today I paid off the last of the money I borrowed from the bank to build the swimming pool. The list of things I did without or gave up doing is long and interesting. I don't miss any of them and probably won't go back to buying, using, or doing them ever again.

POSTSCRIPT: MAY 13, 2010

It was a totally Zen experience to trade Chanel makeup for stuff I buy at the drugstore, to give up massages by treating my back to the long, hard swims in the pool, to stop going out to eat in crowded restaurants and learn to cook vegetables and make my own salads, to "shop my closets" now that the exercise I'm doing every day is keeping me from gaining weight. I don't know if I can prove this but swimming is much better for the way my body looks than the long, hard miles I used to walk and run.

This is just a partial list of how I managed to pay back the bank without feeling deprived. I felt empowered actually. I decided I was secretly related to the "bene Gesserit" women in the Dune books.

Don't dread jumping in the cold water. Just do it and start swimming. Don't care how old your blouse is. Just iron it, put it on, and leave the house.

I wonder if the mall misses me? I bet it does.

Behaviorists, Freudians, Jungians, and Zen: A Short History of a Learning Curve

---

I HAVE HAD MANY GREAT TEACHERS IN MY FORTUNATE LIFE. I had parents who loved me and were busy teaching me everything they knew from sunup to sundown. So maybe I give too much credit to things I learned after I left their care. Perhaps it all happened in childhood and the later lessons were just reminders of things I had already learned but didn't pay attention to until I needed the information as an adult.

I was in psychotherapy for many years. With a great Freudian in New Orleans and later with a Jungian Zen psychoanalyst in Fayetteville, Arkansas. Before those two great adventures I learned to quit drinking from a behaviorist. He was a distance runner who had given up surgery when he had detached retinas. His ways of being a psychiatrist were very close to the way I live my life. I was for many years a distance runner so, of course, we got along. He tried many behavioral tricks to talk me into quitting. The hypnosis failed. Both of us were too hyper for that to work. In the end he gave me a drug called Antabuse. If you drink while it is in your system you will get so sick you think you are dying. I didn't take it for long, just long enough for me to learn to live in a world where everyone drank and there were parties every night without joining in the drinking. It showed me how horribly boring and dumb people become when they drink alcohol. So I quit going to the parties and very easily I never drank again.

The psychotherapy taught me to understand and accept myself. It taught me to believe in my own emotions and ideas. Because of it

I was able for many years to write the exact truth as I saw and experienced it. It taught me how funny we all are, and how influenced by even the best parents in the world. The self cannot develop fully until you can step outside your childhood influences and see the world with your own eyes.

The other great influence on my life has been my thirty-seven-year attempt to learn to meditate. I'm still not very good at it. I can't sit still long enough to sit in zazen. I can control my breathing when I am walking around a room better than when I am alone on a prayer bench. But still I have kept on trying to learn the things that Zen Buddhist masters know. Be here now. Live in the present. When you're hungry, eat. When you're sleepy, sleep.

Knowing how to watch my breath and certain breathing techniques I learned from a CD by Doctor Andrew Weill are the most amazing things I have learned since I was in psychotherapy years ago. You calm yourself. You control yourself. You conquer your emotions. Then you can think straight and help out in emergencies. Then you can work. You can stop the endless fear-filled wanderings of the mind and write a book.

Distance running is a form of Zen. Taking a long brisk walk is Zen. Paying attention to the moment is pure Zen. You can do all of these things without sitting on a prayer bench hurting your knees.

All of these things I learned as an adult are versions of things my parents taught me when I was small.

How to Have a Seventy-Fifth Birthday
Party That Is a Surefire Success

FEBRUARY 20, 2010

I WAS SEVENTY-FIVE YEARS OLD ON FEBRUARY 20, 2010. I usu-ally don't celebrate my birthdays with large gatherings. I like to buy myself gifts all during the month of February instead and be sur-prised by the cards and small gifts children in my family send me by mail. I am happy knowing I am healthy and well and have fifteen grandchildren and two great-grandchildren and have had a long and blessed life.

Usually I like to let my birthday happen as it may, knowing I am going to be glad I am alive and well no matter where I am or who I'm with. Once I gave myself a replica of a statue of Aphrodite from the Metropolitan Museum of Art. Several times I was in New York on business spending glorious afternoons in museums.

Many times I was traveling on my birthday, giving talks at univer-sities. Twice the students found out it was my birthday and gave me wonderful celebrations. In Wilkes-Barre, Pennsylvania, they made me a chocolate cake and gave me a long maroon wool scarf and a pair of pink leather gloves that I still cherish and wear in the winters.

In two thousand and five I was spending the winter holding the Andrew W. Mellon Chair in the Humanities at Tulane University. I was simultaneously holding a chair at Newcomb College in the women's half of Tulane. I chose to have my office in the women's center because so much was going on there, not the least of which was an interesting long-running controversy about how much power Tulane could exert over Newcomb. I had been hearing about this ongoing argument for twenty years since my daughter-in-law is a Newcomb graduate and a fierce defender of Newcomb College's right to be independent from Tulane. Besides, the women's college offered me a much larger office and a twenty-two-year-old computer genius from Chicago to teach me to run my computer. He immediately took me to amazing sites on the computer, such as the then-new Wikipedia, and made running a computer into a maze of intellectual potential I would never have found on my own. It did bother me that the information on Wikipedia was not peer-reviewed and could be augmented by anyone on the site in any way but David Emerson seemed to think that was just part of the fun.

Another thing the women's center at Newcomb College did for me was plan a huge celebration on my seventieth birthday. This was in February before Hurricane Katrina happened in August of the same year and New Orleans was still in full swing as the party capital of the United States.

There were huge signs all over the campus saying A SOUND MIND IN A SOUND BODY, my motto for my visit, and the seminar I arranged for later in the spring. The signs were in Latin and in English and large pins were made and passed out for months. I was deep into yoga practice that year and the center even let me have a yoga demonstration as part of the writing seminar.

The party was in McAllister Hall at Tulane, where I had once been the leader of an anti–Vietnam War demonstration. There were dozens of beautiful white roses, my favorite flower. Many of my grandchildren were there. Later, at the reception, there were three huge cakes, each one more elaborate than the last, including a chocolate Doberge tart from Gambino's restaurant which I consider the meal you order on your deathbed so you won't notice you are dying.

There was a huge crowd at the reading in McAllister Hall and so many people at the reception I didn't have time to eat cake until late that night.

~ ~ ~

With all these lucky birthdays happening without my having to plan them I had not had a birthday party for myself in many years, if I ever had one at all.

But this year, because the young people in my family talked me into being on Facebook, making it easy to send invitations on a whim, I sent out a Facebook feeler saying I was thinking about having a birthday cake with seventy-five candles and seeing if I could blow them all out. I have been swimming twenty laps a day for two years and thought I had the wind to make a run at seventy-five candles, it was worth the chance.

My grandchildren and nieces and great-grandchildren and great-nieces and -nephews began writing back saying they would love to come and watch.

I have a condominium on a beach in Ocean Springs, Mississippi, that is near where many of my progeny live and with the help of a daughter-in-law and granddaughter-in-law the party was set in motion. To make things easy my seventy-fifth birthday was on a Saturday. Our plan was to get everyone there, set the candles on fire and blow them out, then eat the cake. Of course ice cream and carrot and celery sticks would be available. Next, we planned to go down to the beach and build a huge bonfire. My daughter-in-law went to the police department and got the bonfire permit, my youngest son and oldest grandson collected the firewood from all over town and we were set.

My two professional photographer daughters-in-law brought cameras and the party was ready. My granddaughter-in-law delivered the cake and since she is a professional decorator she found long slim candles that are so thin and tall they would fit on a cake. She arranged them in the center of the cake like a sheath of wheat and we set them on fire. It was an inferno! I was surrounded by a seven-year-old boy, two four-year-old boys, a tall, strong thirteen-year-old champion girl swimmer, an eleven-year-old girl star of school musical productions, and several other strong eleven-year-old girls. We could not blow them out. My twenty-eight-year-old physician grandson who is six feet seven inches tall finally leaned in over the smaller grandchildren and managed to deliver the coup de grace to the bonfire. It had been very, very exciting for several minutes with everyone's hair and the whole kitchen area in danger of being ignited.

We scraped tallow off the top of the cake, cut it into pieces and feasted.

By the time we finished the cake and ice cream the sun was going down and the fire on the beach was beginning to burn brightly. It was not a small fire. Ocean Springs is still being rebuilt from Hurricane Katrina so there is always plenty of scrap wood to be found if you know where to look.

All in all it was the best birthday party of my life. Later, to cap off the evening, my eleven-year-old and thirteen-year-old granddaughters and their twin best friends, Laura and Marin, read a long poem they had written about me praising me for not getting old yet.

A good time was had by all and there was plenty of cake left for breakfast the next morning.

I highly recommend CAKE FIRE parties to anyone who is old enough to deserve a sufficient number of candles and their attendant flames. But don't get cocky about being able to blow them all out yourself. Have plenty of children standing by and even an adult or two just in case.

SEPTEMBER 8, 2010

Heaven, A Mystical Experience in Late October in Fayetteville, Arkansas, Or, Why We Need to Write and Read Books Until We Die, Which I No Longer Fear or Dream of Understanding

THIS STORY ENDS ON OCTOBER 29, 2014, WHEN I WOKE AT EIGHT a.m., put on my new running shoes, my autumn running clothes, and walked four miles to Barnes and Noble to finish reading a book that terrified and excited me so much I had to visit the store three times in one week to get up the courage to purchase the book and take it home with me. I could no longer drive to the bookstore, the effect that the book had on me was so incomprehensible I had to walk there. It was perfect weather, sunny, clear, sixty-seven degrees, all the trees between my house and the store were turning bright red and coral and yellow and gold. Purple vines were combing fences. Some of the vines still had small, perfect yellow flowers. From the moment I had opened my eyes that morning I had known exactly where I was going and what I was going to do. I finished reading the first book at ten o'clock and walked home carrying a sack with a bottle of Fiji water and an almond croissant I bought in the bookstore café. I never eat fattening baked goods for breakfast but on this day there were no rules. I was going home and coming back in the car to buy the books, why I don't know.

I studied philosophy when I was young. I read and wrote poetry all my life. I searched for first causes relentlessly. For the last ten years I have been satisfied DNA is all I need to know about first causes, and I still believe that, but DNA is about connections and vast timeless love, which I have just been reminded I am a part, always have been a part, always will be. As we all are whether we know it or not. Writing may play some part in that. Certainly reading and the mystery of books is part of it. This whole experience is so mystical I am being driven to adverbs.

The book is called *Proof of Heaven: A Neurosurgeon's Journey into the Afterlife* by Eben Alexander, M. D. It was written by a scientist and physician who has spent his life operating on the human brain. Harvard, Duke, Brigham and Women's Hospital, Harvard Medical School are all real parts of his vitae. He is the adopted son of a neurosurgeon and the natural son of an astronaut trainee for NASA space missions who later became a pilot for Pan Am and Delta airlines.

Nothing in his scientific life or upbringing prepared him for his weeklong coma from E. coli meningitis of the brain and the weeklong near-death experience he had during that time. There was no discernible brain activity during his coma. The fact that he survived and came back to his full memory and brain activity and surgeon's work is a miracle in itself. Of course he was in the hospital where he worked, being taken care of by his huge loving family and the best physicians and neurosurgeons on the East Coast, none of whom believed he would wake up or live or recover.

In his near-death experience, which he remembers exactly and documented completely as soon as he recovered, he traveled in what we call space and time to what all philosophers and poets for thousands of years have described as heaven. His guide for the weeklong trip was a natural sister whom he had never seen or known as she had died before he was reunited with his natural parents and siblings.

Several months after his near-death experience he saw a photograph of this beautiful young woman named Betsy about whom he had been strangely curious for years.

All of Dr. Eben Alexander's experiences since his near-death illness have continued to be mysterious and deeply meaningful to both his life and work as a surgeon. He has studied and researched everything he can find about such experiences and since he published the first of his two books about the near-death journey to heaven in which his sister guided him to unbelievably beautiful places where he met a being he called Om, having never heard the word before or known that it is the person and place Sanskrit and Buddhism call the highest reach of consciousness and all goodness and kindness and light, he has continued to investigate the phenomena.

There is evil in the world and he could see it as he looked down on the blue orb he knew was his home on earth but goodness was always able to overcome it, if not completely destroy it.

I have talked too long about the book. What I am telling you is not half, not a fraction, of the story this scientist has to tell you. There is a heaven, he concludes, and he finds, especially in the second book, many great thinkers and writers and scientists who also believe that the knowledge we have on earth is nothing compared to what real knowledge and infinity are to those who are no longer bound by a human body and human brain. We know that the brain is only the filter that allows an amount of knowledge a human brain can tolerate to enter our human minds and lives.

Dr. Alexander keeps saying that our language doesn't have the breadth and depth to describe what he experienced.

Here is the reason the book frightened me so much when I picked it up in the bookstore and sat down and started reading. I was reading much, much faster than I normally read. I sat down at a table in the bookstore café and read about a hundred pages in what must have been fifteen or twenty minutes. My brain was racing with excitement and recognition and finally fear.

I couldn't take any more. I went back to the shelf where I'd found the book and put it carefully back in its place and almost ran from the store.

An hour before I went to the bookstore I had been sorting through magazine articles from various times in my adult life looking for essays to put in this book. I got up to stretch my legs and turned on the television to see the latest poll numbers from a United States Senate election I am interested in and a woman on *Fox News* was finishing an interview with Dr. Eben Alexander about his second book. I only heard about five lines of what he said and I put on a jacket and ran to the bookstore to look at the book. All of my behavior was as curious, mysterious, and unusual for me as were the things I had heard Dr. Alexander say.

I have had two near-death experiences of my own that were exactly what he was describing, in the interview, and later in the book. Also, an experience in which my seven-year-old son called out to me for help from ten miles away and the message arrived so perfectly and instantly (from my child to me directly, no phones, no intermediaries) that I stopped in the middle of sitting down at a table in a restaurant on the top of the tallest building in New Orleans and ran from the room and down the elevator and got into the car so fast you cannot imagine it. I yelled at my husband to follow me and he did, he was so caught up in whatever was happening to me he did not question my behavior but followed me and helped me and drove like a madman across New Orleans to where I found my child. He had locked himself out of a mansion on Palmer Avenue by accident and couldn't get back in and was terrified and walked out of the yard and found my car and got into it and was in the back seat hysterical when we drove up and saw him in the car screaming and crying and jumping up and down.

He was spending the night with my husband's parents and had awakened and gone downstairs to get some candy from a bowl on a table and had walked outside to look for me and closed the huge door behind him.

That night, that instant communication and my and my husband's response to it have haunted me all my life. I am as certain of what happened as I am of anything I know. Pierre called to me for help and I heard him and both my husband and I ran and hurried to him so fast it was inhuman. People who spend their lives studying such things call that communication psychic. A psychoanalyst told me many times I am "a good receiver."

Since then I think I know when any of my children are in danger or trouble or unhappy. If I think that, I call them or go to where they are.

From that night, when I was about twenty-eight years old, I have believed that people communicate with each other across space and time constantly, that we know who we can trust, that we know who we should love and I also believe that my parents are somehow still alive and communicate with me. I know that the angels and fairies my mother always told me were looking out for me exist. A fairy for each leaf on every tree. A guardian angel who is always around. I also believe in lucky rocks, lucky charms people give me, and the absolute and inexpressible joy of bringing happiness to other people. Figuring out what they need and giving it to them before they know they need it is the greatest pleasure of my life. I still work at two jobs full time to have the money to fix things for my children or my friends.

The two near-death experiences are the other times when I had a glimpse behind the curtain into the world of unbelievable light and beauty that Dr. Eben Alexander visited for seven days and believes is waiting for us all when we leave our human bodies.

My first near-death experience was in Wyoming, on a two-lane mountain road coming down from the Grand Targhee Ski Resort in the Teton Mountains to Jackson Hole, Wyoming. We were thirteen people in three cars. My older brother and his wife were in the front seat of a diesel Mercedes and my second oldest son and I were in the back seat. My father and mother and five or six of the grandchildren were behind us in a mountain truck with a covered back. It was very late, on the twenty-fourth of December and the sun had already left the mountains but there was enough light left for my one-eyed genius brother to spot an elk on a high place between two mountains. He turned to the back seat to point it out to my thirteen-year-old son and the front wheels of the Mercedes hit a slick spot and the car began to roll down the snow-covered mountain sideways. It moved very fast. I was absolutely certain we were all going to die and I looked at my child and thought, oh, no, he is too young to die. After that all I saw was wonderful white light, brighter than the sun and perfectly beautiful, surrounding myself and the car on all sides, holding us. It was so beautiful and so perfect and my only memory is of light and perfection and beauty. Everything disappeared but that light.

Later, when the car had miraculously banked itself into a stopping point down the mountain and people were there rescuing us and taking us up to the top of the mountain and covering me in blankets and putting me in the back of my father's truck my memories are confused and not as clear. I was never cold, never scared, never worried, it was all all right. Everyone else in the car has clear memories of the rescues but I just remember the light and that I was dying and that it was all right. Except for the moment when I regretted that my son was there.

It was the most real thing that ever happened to me in my life and I have remembered it over and over again when things would be wrong with me or I would have to have surgery. I have had no fear of death since that moment.

A few years later I was on a Delta Airlines jet going from our small airport in Fayetteville, Arkansas, to Atlanta and suddenly the oxygen masks fell. We had lost an engine and the pilot announced we were making an emergency landing in Memphis, Tennessee. The plane went straight down and again I was quite certain I was going to die and again the whole airplane filled with light and it was all absolutely beautiful and perfectly all right and I had no fear. I was sorry I was sitting so far away from the other people but it was all right. It was beautiful and that was that.

In Dr. Alexander's book everything he describes is exactly, as well as our language can express it, as I saw it both of the times I was convinced I was dying.

The tenderness and love that I felt for all the other people on the airplane was still there when we landed. We all stayed very close together after we got off the plane. It was twenty minutes or so before we could leave one another, another very strange phenomena.

An hour later, I boarded a plane for New York City. That flight was difficult. I kept listening to the engines, looking at my watch, I was back in the land of living where we have to be vigilant and aware and make up catastrophes in our brains.

It was late October when I read Dr. Alexander's book, which I have read several more times since then. Now it is mid-December and the world is filled with Christmas cheer. Rejoice, rejoice, Emanuel, is come to thee, O, Israel. I have been in several churches and both times I have felt very close to the people around me, all my fellow human beings longing and searching for light and miracles and signs and wonders, all singing about such searches and believing there was once a time when we were nearer to such divine ideas as virgin births and wise men and stars appearing to lead the way to a better world and a miraculous birth.

I am going to start going every Sunday to either the Presbyterian or the Episcopal Church. My son has won custody of a child who has never been to church and longs to go to one. So we are going to take him but it is really myself I am taking. I want to be among people who believe in things they cannot prove.

Blessings

Christmas Past

IN OCTOBER OF 1705, WHEN HE WAS TWENTY YEARS OLD, BACH traveled three hundred miles across Germany, much of it on foot, to hear Dietrich Buxtehude play the magnificent organ at the Marien-kirche in Lübeck. There were Christmas concerts and a grand concert in memory of Emperor Leopold I. I like to think of the young man walking so many days to hear the aging composer whose work he had studied and played. Perhaps he stopped at inns along the way. Perhaps he slept on the ground, his pack for a pillow, his cloak around him against the cold. October turned into November. The fields and towns, which were covered in gold when he left his home in Arnstadt, became covered with snow. Perhaps he saw such scenes as Monet would later paint in masterpieces like *The Magpie*.

This year I am going to think of Bach's journey as the days lead up to Christmas. I am going to listen to great music as the nights grow longer and colder and the dangerous holidays draw near. Every time I want to turn on the television I am going to listen to Bach and Beethoven and Mozart instead. Instead of concerning myself with riots and earthquakes and plagues I am going to listen to Mozart's *Jupiter* Symphony, or Beethoven's Sixth Symphony, or Bach's Prelude and Fugue No. 1 in C from the *Well-Tempered Clavier*, or the Mass in B minor. Instead of being preoccupied with the chaos of the world, I am going to concentrate on the things that make the world worth saving.

Actually, this is just my latest strategy in a lifelong attempt to escape the celebrations our culture has created to lighten up the winter solstice. I was a loved and indulged child with parents who were married to each other. Still, my main memories of the holidays are unpleasant ones. If I think of Thanksgiving I think of disgusting amounts of fattening foods. I think of the refrigerator stuffed with leftovers and of stacks of dirty dishes. The only Thanksgiving I remember with any real pleasure was when I was in the second grade and had a role in the school pageant. I was a pilgrim and got to sing, "We are little Pilgrim maidens, in our caps of snowy white. We came over on the Mayflower, on a dark and stormy night." Although I liked the pageant, I really wanted to rewrite it. I would have much preferred to be an Indian maiden and get to recite *Hiawatha*.

My memories of Christmas always begin with the trauma of having to keep secrets and the worse trauma of having secrets kept from me. Because of this terrible secret-keeping, there is always a letdown after the presents are opened. "That's all there is?" any child worth his salt will ask. "We've opened everything?" "That's all I got?" Cause and effect, tension and release, simple physics.

The best defense against the holidays is to remember what it is we are really doing: we are trying to lighten up the darkness of winter. That is why I am going to spend the next two months listening to music—to remind myself that the idea is to cheer people up. I no longer need to cheer myself up during the holidays; I have already tried every conceivable way to keep from being depressed, so I have those strategies to fall back on, plus this new one of music.

The main thing I have learned is to stay flexible. I don't have to cook a turkey and make cornbread dressing. I can take everyone out to dinner or go to someone else's house. I can have a simple, elegant meal of vichyssoise and a soufflé. I can fast all day or go for a twenty-mile walk or buy everyone watches that are little automobiles that can be taken off and raced across the table.

By the time my sons were teenagers I had begun to experiment with ways to make Christmas more bearable. My first efforts were feeble and fragmented. I fixated on the tree. I decided it was ridiculous to cut down millions of trees and haul them around the United States and install them in living rooms at a cost of twenty-five dollars to one hundred dollars per household. Millions of dead trees festooned with cheap lights and decorations, sitting forlornly in their plastic holders full of stagnant water.

The first Christmas I rebelled I got a ladder out of the garage and painted it silver and hung it with lights and laid presents on the steps. My youngest son still hasn't forgiven me for that Christmas. On Christmas Eve, he and my husband went out and bought a regular tree and set it up in the dining room and moved their presents in there.

The next year I tried having a live tree. Four men struggled valiantly to carry a huge pot of dirt with a pear-shaped cedar into the house. They got it as far as the front hall and there it sat, looking like a giant cedar Buddha. After Christmas, the men returned and moved it to the side yard, where it promptly died. This cost quite a bit of money and cured me of my tree fixation.

It is not the tree, I decided. It is all the parties and everyone getting drunk. The following Christmas we took the children to the British Virgin Islands to spend the holiday on a sailboat. The downside of this adventure is that my two older sons now live in the islands and I have to travel nine hours to see them. Not to mention worry about them getting skin cancer. There are pitfalls everywhere in the Christmas game.

Another year my brothers and I took all our children to Wyoming to learn to ski. My parents came along, too. Everyone did learn to ski. But the children kept locking themselves in bathrooms to smoke marijuana, my one-eyed brother drove a Mercedes off the road in a snowstorm (causing me to have my first near-death—and only out-of-body—experience), and when I got home from the trip, I learned that I had pneumonia.

In recent years, three Christmases stand out in my mind. When my oldest grandson, Marshall, was five, I was at his house in New Orleans on Christmas morning. As soon as the presents were opened, I kissed my sons and their wives goodbye and, with my grandchild, began driving to my home in Arkansas. By sundown we were in the delta in the middle of a flood. We checked into a hotel in Dumas and spent the evening at the local discount store. Marshall bought a detective set with a secret code concealed in the handle of the gun. He still remembers finding the hidden spring and pulling out the rolled-up piece of paper. He says it was at that moment that he began to want to learn to read.

The next morning we continued on our way. In Alma it began to snow, and we locked the keys in the car at a fast-food restaurant. Three members of the Alma football team came to our rescue and opened the door with a coat hanger.

That night, in my house on the mountain, I began to teach my grandchild to read and write the English language. I still have the scrap of paper on which he wrote, "Today we drove to Grandmother's house."

On another great Christmas, I stayed alone all day and wrote the last chapter of a novel. It snowed that year and I saw a white fox in the yard, although I have never been able to get anyone to believe it wasn't just a snow-covered dog.

Last year was an interesting Christmas. My youngest son, the one who can't forgive me for the ladder, was visiting with a friend just home from Russia. At two o'clock on Christmas Eve we learned that the person who had invited us to Christmas dinner was ill and had to cancel the party. We rushed to the grocery store; we bought a frozen turkey. We threw it into a bathtub and ran cold water on it. We made dressing. We mashed sweet potatoes. We ironed a tablecloth. We stayed up until three in the morning basting that turkey.

By noon the next day we had prepared a feast. Cooking a turkey is not so bad as long as there's some drama to it. Not that it tasted very good or that we ate much of it. Luckily, to make up for that, there were plenty of presents under the artificial, predecorated tree I had ordered from the florist. And best of all, the next day would be December 26 and it would all be over.

Morality, Part I

OLD WOMEN ARE SUPPOSED TO BE GUARDIANS OF THE FLAME. They are supposed to snatch baseball caps from the heads of recalcitrant teenagers and hand glasses of water to weary travelers and know when to use adjectives like disgusting and tacky and revolting and loathsome.

I would have to invent a new world to describe what I just witnessed on the Gulf Coast of Mississippi. I would have to create a word that contained the loss of all responsibility for one's fellow human beings. It would have to imply that the persons to whom the word applied had decided there were no standards of behavior. That thievery and bad karma were their meat and drink, the very air they wished to breathe.

Last Sunday afternoon in Biloxi, Mississippi, across the bay from the beautiful little town of Ocean Springs, where she lives, I took an eight-year-old girl by the hand and went to visit the children's arcade of the Boomtown Casino, one of forty casinos that have opened there in the last few years. Here, at the children's annex of Boomtown, within cigarette smoke of the big casino, is a large hall filled with machines designed to teach children how to gamble. The children put their money into a machine and gambling chips come out. One chip for a quarter. Four for a dollar. Something for nothing. This is also an excellent metaphor for the act of faith that is money.

Once the child has their chips in hand, or in the plastic cups provided for that purpose, they can wander around the floor and choose from a variety of games which cheerfully and matter-of-factly cheat them of their chips. None of the children seem to expect they will actually win the basketball toss, alligator pound, strength test, or roulette wheels. Accustomed to being cheated, they wander from machine to machine putting in their chips and accepting their losses with a sad-eyed resignation. The children are sad. It is Sunday afternoon on the Gulf of Mexico and I am in a room full of sad children carrying plastic cups filled with gambling chips. Occasionally one of the machines pays off, ejects a row of paper coupons which the child can exchange for worthless plastic toys at a counter manned by two overweight young women wearing maid uniforms.

At the back of the hall is a cage where croupiers sell tickets to the VIRTUAL REALITY THEATRE. The tickets cost two and a half dollars. For this amount the ticket-holder is strapped into a chair and rocked from side to side and up and down while watching a screen that distorts his or her sense of balance and orientation. For a flat fee of ten dollars a child can be left all day in the Boomtown Children's Arcade and can ride the VIRTUAL REALITY chairs as many times as they like.

I had a really degrading and dehumanizing experience at Boomtown. Illuminating. I saw white children so fat they had to buy two seats in the VIRTUAL REALITY THEATRE. I saw Afro-American children only five years old being helped to stick their chips in the machines. I saw Asian children sitting strapped into chairs by the roulette wheels. Red and yellow, black and white, all are precious in the Southern Mafia's sight.

I guided my eight-year-old companion, whose name is Aurora, from one machine to the next until she had spent five dollars' worth of chips. I told her the things that five dollars could buy in the real world but she was not interested in my lecture. She knew I wasn't going to give her any more money to stick in the machines and she was mad about that. "This is disgusting," I told her. "This is revolting, loathsome, common, and tacky."

"I want to do the roller coaster ride," she said, referring to the most frightening of the VIRTUAL REALITY programs. "You said you'd let me do it."

"I changed my mind," I told her. "We're going to the park."

An hour later we were in the children's park in Ocean Springs, Mississippi. The park is three acres of land left to the city's children by a gentle patroness who used to be a teacher. There are trees and swings and covered picnic tables. There are trash cans hand-painted with underwater designs by a local artist. There is a gymnasium with a swinging bridge for daredevils. Adjacent to the park is the backyard of Mr. Penny Cates, age sixty-four, who has built along the separating fence a pen in which he keeps a gorgeous fighting cock and two hens. On this Sunday afternoon there were three newly hatched chicks, pecking in the dirt which their mother kept scratching up with her talons.

Aurora stared long and hard into the pen. She was transfixed, as the cock strode and preened and the unchicked hen brooded in the background and the mother hen scratched and the chicks fed. Sunlight fell down between the boards which Mr. Cates has laid across the top to keep children from throwing sticks into the pen. He came walking towards us now, a handsome man with bright red hair, wearing khaki pants and cowboy boots, his body as lithe and straight as a young man's, his wide, freckled hands spread out beside his hips.

"Why did you put these chickens here?" Aurora asked.

"For children to look at," he answered. "People used to fight these cocks. Put razors on their claws and let them fight to the death."

"That's disgusting," Aurora said. "They ought to go to jail."

"He's in molt right now," Mr. Cates added. "You come back in December when his tail is grown back in. He'll be a beautiful sight by Christmas."

"He's beautiful now," I put in. "The ruff around his neck is the prettiest thing I've ever seen. It's very nice of you to keep these chickens for the children. What a nice thing to do."

"They're costing me money every day." Mr. Cates spread his freckled hands and laughed out loud. "But there they are. Come back in two months, when his tail feathers are grown back in."

Aurora stared deep into the cage, coveting the chicks. The mother hen scratched fiercely. Dirt flew out through the chicken wire and landed on our feet. Three little boys came running up. One of them was carrying a package of Cheetos. He stuffed one through the wire. He popped one in his mouth. I wanted to kiss Mr. Penny Cates. I wanted to polish his boots or send him a ten-pound sack of chicken feed or call him things like noble and inspiring and gorgeous and Homo Sapiens Sapiens.

Proving Once Again I Will Do
Anything for My Granddaughters

I NEVER SET FOOT ON A CRUISE SHIP NOR HAD THE SLIGHTEST desire to do so until my granddaughters called one cold January day and asked if I would chaperon their dance team on a five-day cruise to Nassau in the Bahamas. They had been invited to be the entertainment for the last night of the cruise. Their dance lessons are projects I paid for, and have been involved with for many years. I have sat for many hours watching them rehearse and have been the backstage mother for countless Christmas shows and recitals. My granddaughters are fifteen and seventeen years old. Their glorious dancing years are almost over. How could I say no?

So I am going on a cruise. I don't like crowds. I don't like to sleep in strange beds. I'm bored with the Caribbean, but, after all, it is only for four nights and five days. I love my granddaughters and the girls on their team, and I know and admire their dance instructors. I knew I would be in good company. Another thing I have never done is go anywhere with a group of women, but these young women are dancers and athletes. I decided to open my mind and broaden my horizons.

Another thing I don't like to do is live on a boat. When I was younger, my husband and I kept a fifty-foot sailboat in the British Virgin Islands. We would sail it around for weeks on end, usually in the company of our two best friends. I think of that experience as a dreary round of rationed water, canned food and begging to get off and spend a night at Little Dix Bay. The idea of being on a ship with a bed and showers is new to me. "You'll have to get a new bathing suit, Grandmother," the younger girl said to me. "And, of course, a base tan."

In April I ordered a bathing suit from Lands' End and began to lie out in the sun for thirty minutes every day. These preliminary activities changed my personality to such an extent that I was entertaining the idea of buying a flowered dress. I didn't actually buy one, but I tried several on and did buy a tropical print shirt from a 75-percent-off sales rack. In my normal life I do not wear flowered dresses, print shirts, or anything with writing on it. Perhaps the sun was going to my head.

It was around this time that I called the cruise line and upgraded the reservations for myself and the girls. The team had special fares for the cruise, and I had told myself it would be an adventure to travel in steerage, but then thought better of it. "Give me adjoining cabins on the deck where you would book your parents," I told Michael, in the Miami office of Royal Caribbean. "Make sure I can sleep."

Chaperons are supposed to stay in the same room with their charges, but I trust my granddaughters not to get into trouble. Also, their sleep patterns are not in tune with mine. They would be getting up about the time I went to bed for a nap and would want to watch television after I was asleep for the night.

With my base tan, my print shirt, and my upgraded reservations, I decided I was ready for whatever a cruise turned out to be. Stories of cruise ships limping back to port with all the passengers sick with dysentery did cross my mind, and I prepared myself for a certain amount of Disneyland tackiness, but I was ready. I used to scuba dive when we had to fill our own tanks with air and mail the regulators to California to be checked for holes. I figured I could weather a five-day cruise.

The girls, Aurora and Ellen Walker, and I drove to Cape Canaveral on the eve of the cruise. I made everyone go to bed early. Aurora had warned us that we might have to wait in lines to board the ship, and we wanted to be early to avoid the crush. Visions of Ellis Island. I do not stand in lines. There is nothing I want enough to stand in line to get.

I was amazed at the size of the ship. No photograph can prepare you for the size of a cruise ship. We weren't even on the largest one. Royal Caribbean has a class of ships called Voyager that are much larger.

Our voyage began on Sunday. There was no waiting in line. We arrived early, parked the car under a palm tree and were whisked aboard the ship by a polite, helpful crew.

Our cabins were spacious and well-appointed, and the interior was as clean as a hospital. I was breathing sighs of relief.

By noon we were in deck chairs in our bathing suits, putting on suntan lotion and drinking lemonade.

"Ellen Gilchrist," I heard a voice say. It was Donna Burke, the dance troupe's choreographer and leader. "They've put us in the lounge," Donna said. "I can't believe they did this to us."

Sovereign of the Seas has four dance venues. One is a beautifully designed theater with professional lighting and sound. The rest are dance floors in lounges. The British cruise director had reserved the theater for her own revues, in which she stars and which include professional dancers and stand-up comedy routines, replete with bathroom jokes and making fun of newlyweds.

Our dancers were relegated to a dance floor in a lounge.

"It's too small," Donna continued. "There are posts that will make entrances and exits impossible, no dressing rooms."

Donna's aide-de-camp, Kathy Gaye, joined us. "Donna will make it work," Kathy said. "When we were young, we danced on every sort of stage known to man. Donna will find a way."

"I don't know," Donna said. "I can't squeeze a chorus line in between these poles unless I rechoreograph the whole thing."

The three of us stood in a circle, thinking about this bad turn of luck. Then the dancers began appearing all around us in their bathing suits. I have known most of them since they were children and seen them through countless recitals, lost tap shoes, missing props and capes and hats, last-minute lighting and sound problems, and this year, the loss of the lead dancer to an injury during dress rehearsal. The show had always gone on, and it would again.

A band began playing calypso, the irresistible, seductive music of the islands. Lunch was being served, waiters danced by, carrying trays of exotic drinks. Our girls began to dance all around us, first moving in their deck chairs, then standing up and mocking dance moves to amuse one another, then out onto the dance floor, showing off, being silly, having fun.

I started laughing. In a few hours we would set sail for the Bahamas. Carpe diem. Let the good times roll.

I am much too vain to be interested in food. I live on low-calorie, high-protein foods and like to eat the same things day after day. Oatmeal, salads, olive oil, broiled meats, and tofu are the staples of my regular diet. I was so worried about not being able to stick to my regimen on the cruise that I had packed some Luna bars and sugarless bread in my cosmetics kit. I should not have worried. It was possible to eat almost exactly as I do at home. In a group of dancers, my culinary tastes were considered normal. Our Portuguese waiter put up with my ordering broiled salmon every night until the last night. On the last night she threw up her hands and begged me to let her bring me something with a sauce.

My main interest in the meals was in how our girls looked. Every night they turned up looking resplendent in their old prom and homecoming and cotillion tea dance dresses. I do not know how they fit all those clothes into their suitcases, except young girls' dress-up dresses are made of very thin materials now, as you may have noticed.

I had three sons. I lived in a world of baseball caps and football uniforms and athletic shoes. It is the great joy of my older years to watch my granddaughters dress up and put on makeup and jewelry. We are southern women and think of dressing up as an art form.

Before dessert, which most of them did not eat, the girls went back to their rooms to change into clothes more useful for dancing. They went from one dance floor to the next, moving in groups of three or four, dancing to all the different sorts of music being played. They took shortcuts through the casino, where they found me twice putting quarters into slot machines. "I'm appalled that you found me gambling," I said. "This is a foolish, wasteful thing to do. No one ever made money in a casino. Forget you saw me here."

"It's all right," one of Ellen's friends told me. "My mother's been doing it too."

On that first night I wandered around making sure everyone was safe, then went to my cabin and fell asleep. They were too big to fall off the ship; they were policing each other; the bars didn't sell drinks to minors; they were traveling in packs. And I don't like to stay up after eleven o'clock at night.

At dawn on Monday I was awakened by the sound of something dropping near the lifeboat outside my porthole. My years on a sailboat came back in an instant, and I was on my feet going to check the rigging. "Go back to bed," I told myself, but by then I had opened the curtains and seen the Atlantic Ocean, so I put on my running shoes and went to the promenade deck to watch the ship sail into morning.

There were still faint stars but light was beginning to show on the horizon. Early morning has always been my favorite time at sea. I have stood on the bow of a sailboat a thousand mornings, watching light return to the world.

The promenade deck had a walking path that circumnavigated the ship, and I began to walk around it, starting at my muster station and changing directions each time I passed it. There was a man in a deck chair reading a John le Carré spy novel and a woman sitting on a towel in Zen meditation, but aside from that I had the ship to myself. I walked several miles, then began to climb stairs to other decks and explore the ship. I found coffee and cookies near the lounge where we were scheduled to perform. I fixed coffee and walked around the stage looking at the problem. Donna was right. It was too small and the poles on the sides of the stage were in the way for entrances and exits. It was outrageous, but I was sure the cruise director would change her mind now that the girls were aboard and she could see how lovely they were.

I left the lounge and wandered around until I found the real theater. It was exactly what we needed.

I went up to the cafeteria and had breakfast, then returned to the promenade deck to watch the ship drop anchor near our first port of call, a tiny island called Coco Cay, which belongs to Royal Caribbean and is in the process of being developed. The island is very small, and the development is not very far along, but the waters surrounding it are the unforgettable turquoise blue that is one of the great joys of the Caribbean. I have had a lot of fun swimming, scuba diving and snorkeling in that clear blue beauty, and it made me smile for my lost youth to see it now.

I went ashore on the second tender and was greeted by photographers. I posed in my white hat and proceeded to walk around the shopping stalls. There are brightly painted houses and huts with thatched roofs and not much to buy or see. I walked down to the beach bar where the waiters were playing calypso music and opening boxes of plastic cups. One of the waiters caught my eye and began to dance. I began to dance along. We giggled and moved out onto the dance floor. Sell it, I was thinking, forgetting I was the resident grandmother. Show them what you have.

We danced for half an hour. I did not live in the British Virgin Islands all those summers for nothing. I can dance to that music.

"You dance like a girl," the waiter told me when we parted.

"This week I am one," I answered and knew that it was true.

Around eleven I went back to the ship to see if Ellen and Aurora were awake. This became the pattern of the trip. They would stay up late and sleep all morning. I would get up early and wander around or go to the library to read the ship's newspaper. I would eat breakfast alone, take yoga classes or work out in the gym, talk to strangers, watch the ship dock or put down anchors, and in general have a lovely time living my insular, observer's life.

Around noon I would wake the girls, and they would get ready for their activities of sunbathing, rehearsing, dressing up, and wandering around with their friends. Our dancers were in every activity and contest on the ship. They put on acts in the Karaoke Lounge, judged the Sexy Legs contest, took part in line dances, and were constantly being photographed for the cruise video.

So the ship sailed on, as the poets say. I felt lucky and blessed to get to watch these young men and women enjoying their reward for a year of hard rehearsals after school and on Saturday and Sunday mornings. If we had to perform in a lounge, so be it.

My granddaughters' mother is the Yankee daughter of a NASA scientist. She has never understood what Ellen and Aurora and I are doing at Donna's School of Visual and Performing Arts, but she lets us do it nonetheless.

What I was doing on this trip was living vicariously. Sometimes that is as delicious as the real thing.

Our main destination was Nassau. I had gone there in 1958 on my honeymoon and remembered it as a gorgeous, dangerous place with revolution in the air. On that trip I wore green silk and a perfume called L'Air du Temps and walked on the beach at night carrying my high-heeled shoes. In the afternoon we wandered down the main street, which was full of elegant shops and open bars. There was music everywhere, and late at night in the cafes there would always be a moment when the music would change and they would play a song called "Island in the Sun," which was their revolutionary anthem. It is a haunting song, made famous in the United States by Harry Belafonte. I was looking forward to seeing how they had used their independence now that they had gained it. "Oh, island in the sun. Willed to me by my father's hand."

I got up early on Tuesday morning to watch them dock the ship in Nassau. They sailed the ship into the harbor, then turned it around and backed into the docking piers. It was amazing, like watching Gulliver being handled by the Lilliputians. Two blocks away was the city, looking lovely in the dawn. Farther down was the tall, yellow hotel where I had stayed in 1958. At that time it seemed to be far away from the heart of town. Now it was surrounded by buildings, but the beach was still there and I could imagine myself in my green silk strapless dress, high on gin martinis, wading in the surf to show off for my husband.

I dressed up for Nassau and was the first person off the ship when they put down the walkway. It was so early the shops weren't open yet, but I wanted to reconnoiter before I took the girls shopping.

There was not much there. The Nassau I remembered has disappeared. In its place is a dusty tourist town with jewelry stores and streets that need fixing. No matter how hard I tried, I could not find a single place that I remembered.

Still, I did not give up. I went back to the ship at ten and woke the girls and begged them to go shopping with me. They sleepily agreed and we went to town.

"Great," I said. "We'll look for shoes."

We spent two hours shopping but could not find a thing to buy. The merchandise in the shops was covered with dust. We did find some nice jewelry shops, and we found a Versace outlet mall and had fun laughing at the outmoded clothes with thousand-dollar price tags, but in the end we gave up.

The action on Nassau has shifted to neighboring Paradise Island, which has a casino and an aquarium and lots of stalls for hair-braiding.

In the afternoon most of our group went to Paradise Island. Some of them stayed all day and missed the captain's dinner that night.

I did not go with them. I was so disappointed in Nassau I stayed on the ship and read and slept and had a massage and got my hair done in the beauty salon.

Maybe the magic is still in Nassau and I am the one who has lost it. Everyone else had a wonderful time there.

At midnight we began our long, slow voyage back to Florida. We moved through the ocean at ten knots as the last two nights and last day of our journey went by. It would be a busy day for our group. We had to rehearse all afternoon and perform that night. Donna Burke was going into take-no-prisoners mode. While we had been enjoying the cruise, she had been planning how to fit chorus lines onto the dance floor and how to move the entrances and exits around the poles. The other chaperons and I went to work, haranguing the assistant cruise director to move tables and chairs out of the way and to hang lights in the makeshift dressing room.

The girls were as serious now as Donna was, checking and rechecking every piece of costume, helping each other with makeup, slipping into the dressing room without letting the audience see them, all the professional traits Donna has been teaching them all these years.

"Much has been accomplished," I say to myself when I get worried about my progeny and wonder if I have done enough to help them. There are some things I have done that I know were worthwhile. Surely Ellen's and Aurora's dance lessons are in that category.

This day was my reward. At ten that night we took the stage and completely wowed a standing-room-only audience. The dancers did five numbers, including a piece in which Ellen and Aurora had starring roles. When the show was over, the troupe was given a standing ovation.

"Well, honey," a man sitting near me said to his teenage daughter, "I guess you might as well just quit those dance lessons you're taking in Pennsylvania. Compared to this that isn't even dancing."

The other chaperons and I turned and glowered at him, as was proper, but we couldn't help being pleased by the comparison.

I woke the last morning of the cruise and knew I had been made softer by the experience, kinder, less critical. I loved the silly cruise. I loved the multinational crew; the Indians, Bahamians, Englishmen, Portuguese, Norwegians, Italians. I had not gained an ounce and my fingernails had grown half an inch, proving once again that housework ruins manicures.

Disembarking was easy. By ten we had stuffed our luggage into the trunk of my car and begun our six-hundred-mile drive home. I was even looking forward to that. These years when I can have my granddaughters to myself are almost gone. I am too smart not to treasure them while I can.

As soon as we were on the highway, the girls went to sleep and slept most of the way. Is there anything a grandmother likes more than her granddaughters asleep beside her, completely exhausted from dancing the nights away?

On Becoming an Ancestor

I AM A BETTER GRANDMOTHER AND GREAT-GRANDMOTHER THAN I was a mother because I know more than I did when I was young. I am more outer directed. I understand my place in the universe, and, although I always searched for first causes and wondered at and loved life, I didn't really understand what life is. It is the wonder of DNA that makes me get up at four-thirty in the morning and travel on small, dirty airplanes to the Mississippi coast so I can be there when the little children get out of their parents' automobiles and come running in the door to hug me and give me viral colds they picked up at their schools and start asking me in conspiratorial voices if we can go to Wal-Mart and the Dollar Store to buy useless plastic toys made in China. My condo on the beach contains all the Barbie furniture recently featured on television. I even have a real light green sofa and chair and ottoman almost identical to the ones containing the most lead in the television warnings. We keep the doll furniture on a high shelf so the two-year-old towheaded boy won't chew on it. He loves the girls' dollhouses. He likes to put plastic turkeys in and out of the plastic oven. After he puts one in he sits and watches the oven with a serious expression on his face.

My joy at the children's arrival rises to euphoria when they run into the kitchen and check the refrigerator to make sure there is plenty of chocolate pudding we can eat as soon as we can get rid of their parents. They also want to be sure there is plenty of Quaker Oatmeal Squares cereal and high fat milk and Chicken Lean Cuisine. We don't like complicated meals at my grandmother house. It takes up too much time from playing with the plastic toys we already have and plotting to get more without raising their parents' hackles and going to the beach and trying out the new post-Katrina pier and daring our bodies against the possible jellyfish in the Mississippi sound and, God forbid, God forgive me, watching videos. There's a new one the preteen girls and I love. It's called *The Pacifier* and I highly recommend it if you like a good laugh and like to see bad little boys put in their places by little girls who have been trained in the martial arts. The small boys just keep on liking *Scooby Do*. Their parents are so sick of *Scooby Do* we have to keep the volume very low until they leave the premises.

It occurs to me that one reason I am a better grandmother than I was a mother is that I have more money. I always liked to buy books and toys for children and indulge them but now I can do it on a larger scale. Another thing I love to buy are beautiful clothes. My older grandchildren are wonderful to shop with. My oldest grandson is six foot seven inches tall. When he had to have his first tuxedo there were none to rent long enough for him so I took him to the Beau Rivage Casino and bought him one at the Armani boutique. His mother just shook her head. Nine years later he still wears it, it still fits, and he still looks grand in it. He was going to the prom with an older girl who is now his wife and the mother of my great-grandchildren. I know when to hold them. I know sure bets when I see them and I back winners.

Another unending thrill is taking my two oldest granddaughters shopping for expensive blue jeans. The oldest is six feet tall and thin and gorgeous with wild red hair. The second one is five seven and has her mother's dark hair and my dark brown eyes. They both have exquisite taste and look wonderful in clothes. I also take them all to bookstores. I am blessed in that my sons marry women who love books so the children actually read. Is this also DNA? Sometimes I wonder.

Another good thing about having enough money is that I don't like to be left alone with small children after dark. Especially more than one small child from the same family. I CANNOT STAND

SIBLING RIVALRY. I rail against it, but cannot stop it. It is one of the most powerful forces in the universe as the authors of the Holy Bible know. The story of Cain and Abel gets played out every day and night in every household in the world, not to mention politics and war.

I especially do not like to be left alone with small children after nine o'clock at night, which is my bedtime. Thanks to not being poor I have developed a strategy to deal with this problem which still allows their parents to stay out late with their friends. I have found a beautiful, strong teenage girl named Rachel Picard who is always saving up money to go to church camp in the summers. She has three younger siblings and can deal with bedtime fears and sibling rivalry like a professional. I hire Rachel to help me and she takes over when I fall asleep.

I have learned a lot from watching her interact with small children. She is strict and no-nonsense like the marine officer who babysits in *The Pacifier*. She does not beg them to stop fighting. She orders them to stop fighting. She does not beg them to get in bed. She puts them there and tells them to stay put.

It amazes me that it took me so long to think up getting babysitters to help me with grandchildren. It is the absolutely best idea I have had in years.

I don't think I was ever very good at disciplining children or making them mind. It is a gift I do not have. As I told my friend Molly Giles, "I was always putty in their hands but now I am their slave. I would always have killed or died for my children but I did not know why when I was young."

"Your children are not your children," the great philosopher Kahlil Gibran wrote. "They are the sons of daughters of life's longing for itself. They come through you but not from you. They dwell in the house of the future, which you cannot visit, not even in your dreams."

What does that have to do with adoring your grandchildren and great-grandchildren? Everything. It is about loving life itself, about watching the unfolding and coming into maturity of your own self and your parents and grandparents and great-grandparents. DNA is especially easy to spot when you have redheaded children. This strange recessive gene has given me four granddaughters with brilliant red hair of different shades. Beauty, power, order, the amazing intelligence and mystery of DNA, the wild order of the chromosomes. The apple does not fall very far from the tree, my daughter-in-law Rita loves to say.

You bet it doesn't. So maybe I adore these children because I like myself. Maybe I'm a better grandmother and great-grandmother than I was a mother because I'm more content. Whatever life is, I love being here. If it ends, so what? All that DNA is out there replicating and expanding and becoming new people who like to shove turkeys in and out of ovens as much as I once did.

I have not even mentioned the wild joy I take in watching small children learn THE ENGLISH LANGUAGE. Hearing them sing songs I once sang, read books I once read, make jokes, ask endless questions.

When one of the parents of a young child calls to catch me up on things the questions I ask are, what is he saying? What does he call you?

Children take themselves seriously. We have a two-year-old who won't sit in high chairs or any sort of device made to make him able to reach the table. He is a player. He doesn't sit on baby seats. So we just let him sit on regular chairs and watch as he goes to the elaborate trouble of reaching up to get a spoonful of cereal. He manages to do it. This amazes me so much that I wake up in the middle of the night thinking about it. How did he figure out that sitting in a high chair made him less of a player? Everyone says his brother must have told him so but I do not believe it. I think he just figured it out. We have no idea how smart small children are because they cannot talk.

~ ~ ~

On the day my first grandchild was born I looked at him and realized that I would never fear death as long as he lived. When his wife gave birth to his first child I looked at him and said, "Well, I'm in the gene pool for another hundred years." Since he shares my imagination and sense of humor he knew what I meant. "Thanks," I added. "Don't mention it," he answered. "Courtney did the heavy lifting."

There is so much going on that we don't understand. When I looked at my first grandchild and knew, in a blinding illumination, that I would never die, maybe that was a glimpse behind the veil of all we do not know about chemistry and biology and connections.

I don't think you have to have children to share in this wonder. We are all part of the great gene pool of our species. If I were a Zen master I might be able to see deeper than that, might know connections that are vastly wider and infinite.

For now, for this life, I'll just go on being grateful for this smaller knowledge. And for the luck that put me here and has kept me here long enough to learn a little about love.

JANUARY 2008

Grandmother, Great-Grandmother, What Next?

I NEVER DREAMED I WOULD LOVE MY GREAT-GRANDCHILDREN AS much as I love my grandchildren. I never knew they would capture my imagination and attention. I thought that no one could ever love anyone again as much as I love my grandchildren. And yet here they are, a four-year-old boy named Marshall and a two-year-old named Garrett and they have stolen my heart.

I think a great deal about children and grandchildren, about DNA and how the recessive gene for red hair keeps creeping in, even in families where neither the mother nor the father has red hair. It's a marker, as is the powerful personality that always accompanies it in my family.

I have a lot to think about. I have three sons, fifteen grandchildren and four great-grandchildren. "Hostages to fortune," Francis Bacon called our progeny. But they are so much more than that. They are our riches, our gifts to the earth, our endless sources of curiosity. The things that happen as children grow into adults and the things they say when they begin to talk are the most amazing and unimaginable things in the world. The red-headed Garrett, at eighteen months, just said his first sentence. It was a question. We were walking up to my front porch. The front door was being guarded by a huge green and yellow grasshopper. "What's the bug doing here?" Garrett asked. We all stood still. We didn't know he could talk and here it was, a complete English sentence with all the words in the right place and the attitude and gestures to accompany it. A great Shakespearean actor could not have delivered the line with more perfection.

Flash That Light Over Here is the title of a mystery novel his father started when he was eight. I asked him if I could borrow the title but he said no, he would just save it for his own book.

I made a copy of the title, *Flash That Light Over Here*, and rolled it up like a tiny scroll and put it inside a shell that sits over a pond in my house. A thousand times I have been cheered up by opening the shell and reading the title. What a title! What a great idea! What a wonderful life I have led since my grandchildren started being born. They live all over the world, in Denmark and the Virgin Islands and Germany and Australia. But they are there, my beautiful gene-bearers, sending me postcards and letters and lately, Facebook messages. Because so many of them are far away I have had to learn to use a computer. This has been a boon to my colleagues at the University of Arkansas.

I am a better grandmother than I was a mother because I have had a lifetime to watch children grow into adults. I know that what I see when they are six months old is what I will know when they are twenty and thirty and forty. It is amazing how the personalities are stamped on the face and shown in the body language. It is amazing how much you can know about a person from the moment they are born. I do not need scientists to tell me anything about DNA. I have been watching it play out in its mysterious patterns for fifty-five years in the lives of my children.

The amazing thing is how much like my children their children are, whole personalities passed down from uncles and grandparents also. This may be because my sons married women who are like our family, not completely but basically. I received an email yesterday with a photograph taken in my son's farmhouse in Denmark. They have rebuilt the kitchen and living areas of the house. It looks like something I would build, very clean, very orderly, very simple, plain and elegant. Are tastes also inherited? I'm beginning to wonder.

Anyway, I like to play with children more than I did when I was young. I like their company. I see their points of view. And, of course, they go home sooner or later so I never get tired of them.

Postscript: More Miracles, April 22, 2015

I HAVE TWENTY-ONE PROGENY BUT I HAD NEVER WITNESSED A
live birth. My own three were Caesarean sections and I've never had
the courage to even watch a movie or television program of what happens when a woman delivers a baby into the world.

Since all three of my children are males none of my grandchildren
or three great-grandchildren have ever been born to a woman who
was my blood kin. I have loved these women for the children they
gave my family but I have never been deeply involved in the pregnancy or the delivery. Selfishly I let their mothers and grandmothers
carry that burden of worry and love.

I have eight wonderful granddaughters and I have told the oldest
ones for several years that if they don't get pregnant by the time they
are thirty years old I want to bribe them to have some eggs removed
and put into freezing storage. It wasn't a joke, although they always
laughed and acted like it was one. I was ready to make the bribe an
offer they couldn't refuse.

Last year, when she was twenty-nine years old, my oldest, tallest,
redheaded granddaughter and her husband, Sean Perkins, decided
to begin a family. Her name is Ellen Gilchrist Walker Perkins. She is
my namesake as well as the oldest granddaughter.

None of this had anything to do with my threats to bribe her to
freeze her eggs. Their decision was their deep love for one another
and their combined love for other people and animals of all kinds.

I followed the pregnancy from Fayetteville for the first four
months, vitally interested in every visit to the doctor, a monumentally

wonderful and expert gynecologist, Dr. Hope Ruhe. By the time I met Dr. Ruhe I had heard her advice so many times (secondhand from Ellen) that I thought she was an old friend.

In December I applied for an unpaid leave of absence from my work at the Writing Program in the English Department of the University of Arkansas and drove down to my house on the Mississippi coast to be near New Orleans and my expectant granddaughter.

My house is on a small beach only eighty-nine miles from New Orleans and is in the town where Ellen grew up and lived until she went to New Orleans to college. Her home here was destroyed by Hurricane Katrina so my place has become the spot where the grandchildren who lived here come to see old friends, attend weddings and baby showers and funerals and just to stay near the beach where they played all their lives. Also, it is a good place to get away from the craziness of New Orleans at times like Mardi Gras and Jazz Fest.

The pregnancy went by like a dream. There was morning sickness and fear of ruining her beautiful tall thin body but she kept on with her work of teaching yoga and did exactly what the doctor and the Internet demanded, no alcohol, a careful diet, vitamins and calcium pills, and whatever else was suggested by a daily pregnancy site she watched on her computer. I thought some of the warnings on the site went a bit too far but if I had been having a baby in 2015 I would have been watching it too. In the 1950s I was surrounded by aunts who had given birth, and cousins and friends and a sister-in-law so I got lots of advice, most of it sound but some of it silly. Everyone said if you want the baby to come on out you should run up and down the stairs a lot so I did that and my first child was born a month early coming one foot first, which is why I had to have a Caesarian section at a time when they cut from side to side through the large muscle groups to get to the uterus. After that all the following pregnancies have to be Caesarians or the muscles might tear.

Ellen's Internet advice had been peer-reviewed and she was dedicated to do this pregnancy and birth to perfection. Her husband was so into it he gained a few pounds and showed other signs of being deep into the process with her.

From the beginning Dr. Ruhe had predicted the birth to be on April 21, a prediction she told me later almost never was this specific.

On April 17 Ellen and Sean drove the ninety miles to my house to spend the weekend and get some sun and sand and attend the funeral of a much-too-young mother of one of Ellen's close friends. My youngest son, Pierre, and his wife, Natalie, and five-year-old daughter, Josephine, came over also to help watch and wait. The soon-to-be-parents were getting ready, and so was Sunny Louise. Ellen was dilated one centimeter. She had seen Dr. Ruhe that morning who said the baby probably wouldn't be there until the following week.

Ellen went for short walks, but for the first time in her life didn't seem to really want to exercise. We tried watching *Downton Abbey* but the men got bored so we watched the Discovery Channel and saw a fabulous film about the building of the Roman aqueducts in the third century B.C. Pretty amazing creatures, human beings. All the while Sunny was kicking the hell out of Ellen's liver with her very long and, it turned out, strong legs, and moving nearer and nearer to her destiny with the sun for which she would be named.

At ten that night I wanted to go to sleep but before I went upstairs I said we had to have a plan in case the water broke while we were sleeping. Ellen said she would go five miles away to the Ocean Springs hospital and would not try to make it back to New Orleans but she hated not to have Dr. Ruhe there.

I managed to sleep most of the night, as did most of the party and at ten the next morning Ellen and Sean started driving back to New Orleans.

The excitement was building. The plot was thickening. I went around "praying without ceasing," advice from the Old Testament which I had been remembering from something I heard on television or read in a book. It is from II Thessalonians but is also somewhere in St. Paul. I first learned it from a book by J. D. Salinger called *Franny and Zooey* which I have read six or seven times and am going to read again this week. Between "praying without ceasing," yoga breathing, wishing on stars and being eternally grateful for the strength and health of my beloved grandchild I made it until Sunday afternoon when I called and Ellen told me she was having contractions. The next morning she saw Dr. Ruhe and was told to go home until they became stronger and closer together. It was happening. Om Mani Padme Hmm, I kept repeating and started packing a suitcase and carrying things out to the car. "You don't have to come yet," Ellen told me at six o'clock Sunday afternoon, but the only reason I didn't start driving that moment was that eighty-year-old women really shouldn't drive at night.

Early the next morning I put gasoline in the automobile, threw clothes in the car, called and got reservations at my favorite New Orleans hotel which is only one block away from Touro Infirmary, the hospital where Ellen was born thirty-one years ago this August first. It was a miracle of another order that they found me a room at the beginning of the first weekend of Jazz Fest. Some dear soul somewhere cancelled their reservations at the exact moment I called, in case you want to call that a coincidence. I'm living too high right now to doubt luck and divine interference if you've been good enough and been "praying without ceasing."

At ten o'clock I was halfway to New Orleans and called Ellen's brother, my physician grandson, and he told me that Ellen was in a delivery room, had already had an epidural and to drive carefully because the baby wasn't expected until the afternoon.

I drove eighty but I was extremely careful, hands on the wheel, Bach on the stereo, eyes on the road, being terribly polite to other drivers but moving on.

I got to the hospital at eleven-fifteen, found the room, washed my hands for about fifteen minutes, and went to sit on the couch beside my grandson-in-law.

Ellen was in no pain, a registered nurse as tall as Ellen was in attendance and she was turned on her side waiting and resting before the big show.

I don't think I had ever been this excited in my life, I kept thinking about the three times my own mother had to drive or fly to where I was having a baby. Her love and devotion and attention were with me. The look on her face when I would see her was the look I was wearing. This was happening to me, now, to my own flesh and blood.

This wasn't about me in any way. This was Ellen and Sean and Sunny's date, their production, their magnificence.

In a short time Dr. Ruhe came in and I met and thanked her and she turned to Ellen and said, "Are you ready to get into position and push that baby out?"

"Oh, yes," Ellen said, and I stood at the back of the room and watched the amazing expertise that the RN and doctor used to position Ellen's long legs and arms so that she could use her deep muscles to push Sunny out into the light.

It was timeless and amazing. Sean and I sat for awhile on a bench with our backs and arms pressed so tightly against each other we might have been in a rugby scrum.

Finally, at Dr. Ruhe's urging, first I, and then he moved a little nearer and stood behind the operating table and watched as Ellen pushed and the doctor and nurse coached and praised her and the head would appear about an inch, then go back in, then reappear.

Finally, in one long series of about twenty deeply held breaths and huge efforts on Ellen's part, the head came all the way out, face up and so quickly you couldn't count to one the shoulders and long body and longer arms and legs. It was the most amazing thing I have ever witnessed. They handed the long beautiful baby girl to Ellen and she began to croon to her and sing her a song as old as the human race.

Such joy, such love and pleasure all over the room, such never-to-be-forgotten pleasure. As Edna St. Vincent Millay wrote, "A memory, never to be bartered against the hungry days."

I am definitely the luckiest woman in the world and every now and then I have the luck to be in the exactly right place at the exactly right moment with the exactly right people.

So I would like to end this book with what Peter Brook called "[a] clear, accurate, precise reflection from which we cannot tear our eyes away."

He was praising the work of William Shakespeare, but I believe you always need the bard in times of great joy or sadness.

Read on if you dare. No one will let me tell them about the dazzling biology I witnessed after Sunny Louise was safely snuggled in her mother's arms.

The only people who can bear to hear this are women who have witnessed it or done it. Attached to the baby was a huge umbilical cord about two inches in diameter and unbelievably complicated and made of materials I'm certain no one could duplicate in a laboratory. Many blood vessels and arteries and layers of clear materials as soft as silk. Dr. Ruhe told me to touch it. It was amazing, so pliable and wildly beautiful. She pulled it out of Ellen's body, foot after foot of it. Not at all like the small hard tubular thing I had imagined an umbilical cord to be. It should have a better name, something like miraculous life-giving creation. At the end of the long cord was the placenta, large and flat and many layered and softer than the softest thing I have ever touched, huge and heavy and not at all bloody or useless now that Sunny no longer needed it. Indwelling, you might call it, or Miraculous Creation Baby Carrier.

I didn't want it to be thrown away or discarded. I liked it so much I wanted to keep it in the room for awhile or send to a place where scientists could recycle it into a new medicine that would cure cancer or tuberculosis or depression or meanness or refusal to understand the wonder of the world of living things.

I moved back while Dr. Ruhe carefully stitched up a place where Sunny's head had torn a few small places in my precious granddaughter's body. They were very careful, small stitches that were made with a material which the body will reabsorb as soon as the incredible human immune system sews itself back together with the real stuff it makes for that purpose.

What a day, what a long, wonderful, lucky day. I'm glad I waited until I was eighty years old to view this wonder. I might not have been smart enough to appreciate it when I was younger and not as open to miracles or willing to know one when I was allowed to witness it.

Hooray for Everything,

ELLEN LOUISE GILCHRIST
APRIL 25, 2015